HOME UNIVERSITY LIBRARY
OF MODERN KNOWLEDGE

BELGIUM

By R. C. K. ENSOR

LONDON

WILLIAMS & NORGATE

HENRY HOLT & Co., NEW YORK
CANADA: WM. BRIGGS, TORONTO
INDIA: R. & T. WASHBOURNE, LTD.

HOME
UNIVERSITY
LIBRARY
OF
MODERN KNOWLEDGE

Editors :

HERBERT FISHER, M.A., F.B.A., LL.D.

PROF. GILBERT MURRAY, D.LITT., LL.D., F.B.A.

PROF. J. ARTHUR THOMSON, M.A., LL.D.

PROF. WILLIAM T. BREWSTER, M.A. (Columbia University, U.S.A.)

NEW YORK
HENRY HOLT AND COMPANY

BELGIUM

BY

R. C. K. ENSOR

SOMETIME SCHOLAR OF
BALLIOL COLLEGE, OXFORD

LONDON
WILLIAMS AND NORGATE

First printed Spring 1915.

CONTENTS

*Similar volumes of kindred interest have already been
published in the Home University Library:*

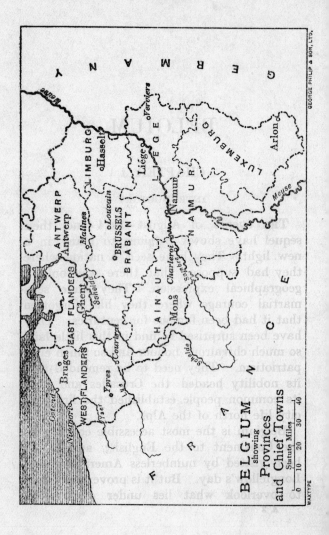

BELGIUM
showing
Provinces
and Chief Towns

Statute Miles
0   10   20   30   40

GERMANY

FRANCE

Namur

LUXEMBURG

Arlon

LIÈGE

Liège

oVerviers

LIMBURG

oHasselt

Meuse

NAMUR

ANTWERP

Antwerp

oLouvain

BRUSSELS

BRABANT

Malines

Ghent

Scheldt

HAINAUT

Charleroi

Mons

Sambre

EAST FLANDERS

Bruges

oCourtrai

Scheldt

WEST FLANDERS

Ostend

oYpres

Yser

Nieuport

Ostend

WAXTYPE

GEORGE PHILIP & SON, LTD.

BELGIUM

CHAPTER I

INTRODUCTORY

THE events of August 1914 and their sequel have shown Belgium to many in a new light. They have seen a nation where they had supposed that there was only a geographical expression. They have seen martial courage where they had forgotten that it had been famous for centuries. They have been surprised to find in this little land so much chivalrous honour and so much civic patriotism. They need to be reminded that its nobility headed the Crusades and that its common people established the first free city life north of the Alps.

Belgium is the most accessible country on the Continent to the English; and it has been visited by numberless Americans since Longfellow's day. But it is proverbially easy to overlook what lies under one's nose.

A 2

Those of us who have long been aware that Belgium is something more than a collection of old buildings and Old Masters, or a stopping-place on the journey to Germany or Switzerland, can but welcome the new interest which is being taken in her by the wider public on both sides of the Atlantic. For she is worthy of it. The episode which the world admires and pities is not an historical accident, ennobling by chance the record of an ignoble people. If under the ordeal they have acted greatly, it was because they had greatness in them.

Anyone studying the Belgians for the first time must beware of mixing condescension with his interest. He will do well to grasp four facts about them as early as possible. They are a nation. They are an old nation. They are a proud nation. They are a nation which has a good deal to teach as well as to learn.

They are a nation; even though they have no national language. A hasty critic once described them as a " fortuitous concatenation of mongrels—Latin mongrels talking bad French, and Teutonic mongrels talking bad Dutch." Undoubtedly they are, like the English, of hybrid origin. Undoubtedly Belgium, like England, has been a meeting-

point between the French language and
culture and the Low-German language and
culture. In the one country, separated by
the sea both from France and Low-Germany,
the languages fused and formed the hybrid
speech in which this book is written. In
the other they remained distinct. But in
both a nation was formed, and exists.

They are an old nation. The political
union in West Belgium between the Flemings
of Flanders and the Walloons of Hainaut,
and that in East Belgium between the
Flemings of Brabant and the Walloons of
Limburg, Namur, and Luxemburg, were being
perpetually wrought, unwrought, and wrought
again in the three centuries between 1050 and
1350, during which the Norman and French
dynasties consolidated the kingdom of
England and Wales. The combining of the
two combinations, that is to say, of all Belgium
except Liége, dates from the fifteenth century;
and it has never been broken since. Through
prosperity and adversity (and adversity is
sometimes the more consolidating of the two)
all Belgians, save those of Liége, have been
united under the same governments for nearly
five hundred years. There are not many
European nations whose people can claim
as much.

They are a proud nation. How should they not be? From the time when the Walloon dynasty of Charles Martel and Charlemagne relaid the foundations of settled life in Europe, down to the time when Antwerp was the shipping metropolis of the world, theirs was always the most civilised country north of the Mediterranean watersheds. If they subsequently endured for three centuries such miseries at the hands of foreigners as not even Italy has suffered, it was their misfortune, not their fault. If they survived; if they preserved through the fiery trial not only their national life but their national love of art, industry, and liberty; if, starting behind all the Western nations eighty-five years ago, they have since reached the very front rank in the rivalries of peace and progress, can they be expected to like hearing their behaviour in the European War praised as if it was the first title to respect that they had ever earned?

They are a nation, which has a good deal to teach as well as to learn. Look, for example, at their constitution. Great Britain can learn from Belgium that it is possible to take ancient liberties, embodied in venerable charters and century-old customs and understandings, and to codify them into a clear logical modern document, legible for all and almost insusceptible of doubts, without destroying their sanctity and efficacy in the process. The United States can learn that it is possible to have a written constitution, and a Judicature which can invalidate laws conflicting with it, and at the same time to have a Legislature which never passes such laws. Look, again, at their industry and thrift. Eighty-five years ago they were poverty-stricken; even in the 'forties and 'fifties it was common to compare Flanders with Ireland. Now for many years theirs has been the one nation in the world besides those old-established bankers, Britain, France, and Holland, which has a sufficient surplus of capital beyond its own requirements to be a large lender to other countries. Look at the unrivalled system of transit and transport facilities, which the Belgian State has developed, with its network of railways, light railways, canals, and ship canals. Or look at its attempts to deal with the housing problem—perhaps the most successful made in any European country.

The present volume will have fulfilled its purpose, if it enables some of its readers to realise the national character and achievements of the Belgian people a little better

than they have done hitherto. It makes
no pretence of being an exhaustive social
study of modern Belgium; nor does it pre-
sume to throw on its history any lights
which have not been thrown before. It is
not meant as a gossiping guide-book; still
less as a statistical abstract. Books filling
all of these rôles with varying degrees of
success already exist; and the present
moment would be a peculiarly unsuitable
one for adding to their number when Belgium
is nearly all in an enemy's hands, when her
libraries and public offices are inaccessible,
when her Government and her Press is in
exile, when her leading citizens are scattered
over half the countries of the world, and when
the whole of her internal activities—industrial,
administrative, intellectual—are either in a
state of suspended animation or in one of
diversion and abnormality. In the following
pages frequent use is made of the present
tense. The reader is informed regarding
this, that, or the other feature of Belgian life
or administration, that it " is." Let him
take note here, once and for all, that in no
case is the tense meant to indicate whether
or not a thing still " is " under war conditions. " Is," in every case not otherwise
shown, means " was when the European

War broke out "; and in most cases let us hope that it means " will be again when the war is over." To avoid endless tiresome circumlocutions we are bound to express ourselves thus; and if the phraseology of convenience happens also to be that of faith, it is none the worse on that account. The present writer does not for a moment believe that Belgium can be obliterated. No one does who has been connected with the country for any length of time. If it were possible to destroy the people's nationality and their determination to live their own life in their own way, they would have been destroyed long ago, between 1555 and 1830.

While a bulky new study of the country could not profitably be undertaken in such circumstances, the case seems different with an attempt to portray it in brief compass by the aid of existing materials. The moment is favourable for this, not merely because the war has made Belgium conspicuous, but because whatever else it may do for her, it marks an epoch. In the eighty-four years since she won her independence, her progress was continuous. There were developments, but no break. The war is such a break; and just as we may care in the life of an

individual to have portraits of him as he
appeared when he left school, or when he
married, or when he entered Parliament,
so there may appear some special reasons
for attempting to place on record the portrait
of a nation, as on the eve of one of the greatest
crises in its career it appeared to a sympathetic
observer.

The first chapter deals with the influence
of geography on the character and destinies
of the Belgian people. It would be difficult
to name any nation in whose history this
has been a more important or more constant
factor. The second chapter describes some of
the more general characteristics of the people
themselves, particularly those of race and
of long-inherited sympathies, antipathies,
traditions, and ways of life. Thirdly, the
reader must appreciate at least the outline
and the main bearings of those glorious
epochs in the history of the Low Countries,
with which every educated Belgian is familiar,
and of which he has the right to be proud.
Fourthly, we trace the story of the evil
centuries, when Belgium was the " cockpit
of Europe." Without this, it is not possible
to realise what a terrible necessity lies upon
her to maintain that neutrality, which Dr.
von Bethmann-Hollweg described on the

outbreak of war as a phrase. For her, neutrality and independence are indissolubly bound together. Once she "gave a passage" to foreign troops from any side, her independence would be gone. Since she had allowed her unique strategical position to be used by others with impunity, none of her neighbours would be content for her to remain the trustee of it; each would be compelled in self-defence to seek control of it. She would not only lose freedom in the process, but would sink back into being a "cockpit" for an indefinite future.

Our fifth chapter deals with the establishment of Belgian independence in 1830–31–39. What should be specially noticed here is that the Belgian nation was not, as is sometimes foolishly said, an artificial creation of the Powers. The Powers were indeed guilty of such an artifice; but it was in 1814–15, when they created the United Kingdom of the Netherlands; and that was the very thing against which the Belgians rebelled. For the formation of their own national State, nobody but themselves was responsible. It originated spontaneously in the will of the people, and is entitled to whatever respect that origin merits. The action of the Powers was limited to putting a certain restraint

on the efforts of their own creature, the
Dutch King, to regain his position, and to
lopping off some pieces of self-freed Belgium
for his consolation and appeasement.

The later chapters give some description
of the constitution, the party politics, the
social conditions and agencies, the art, and
the literature of the modern kingdom. The
principle adopted in the political and social
chapters has necessarily been to direct attention to only a few of the more important
issues and developments, with preference for
those which seem either to be most typical
of Belgium or to be most intrinsically worthy
of notice by an English-reading public.
Only people who suppose that Belgium is
a " little " country and must therefore have
few difficulties and differences, will imagine
that this sort of selection is easy, or can be
performed to the satisfaction of the selector.

The reader will find nothing on two subjects on which he may have expected information. One is the personal history of
the three kings. The other is the Congo.
The omissions are intentional. Our subject
is Belgium; and though the remarkable
personalities of Leopold I, Leopold II, and
Albert I have all exercised a powerful influence on the country, it has in a sense been

external. The reigning family is not, of course, Belgian by origin; and the very great ability which its princes have shown now for three generations has nothing very Belgian about it. Nor was there anything Belgian in the vices and egotisms which were so strangely assorted in Leopold II's character with the highest qualities of foresight, enterprise, and will, and which he displayed on the same colossal scale and with the same indifference to opinion. In England, at any rate, there has been far too common a tendency to talk about Belgium as if it were an annexe to Leopold II and the only important event in its history were that monarch's acquisition of the Congo. The prominence of the present King in his country's fight against aggression is another matter. His greatness and the country's are one; and when it is time—which it is not yet—to write seriously the story of the war as it affects Belgium, his name will lead all the rest. It is probably true, as a Socialist deputy is reported to have said after three months' war, that if Belgium were made a Republic to-morrow and the people had an absolutely free choice of President, they would elect King Albert by a vast majority. It would never have been true of Leopold II throughout his long reign; and not often true of Leopold I before that.

Regarding the Congo, this much may be said. The entire credit (and it is much) for acquiring it and taking the first steps to civilise it belongs to Leopold II alone. So does the entire discredit for the abuses which eventually sprang up under his sway. The Belgian nation had no more to do with the one than with the other. It was a single man's enterprise. It was, of course, the case that King Leopold's dual sovereignty put the Belgian nation into an increasingly difficult position. She would have extricated herself earlier if it had not been for the strong will of the King, the weakness of the then Premier, Count Smet de Naeyer, and, one must add, the extravagances and injustices of the English agitation. Since, however, the transfer was effected in 1908 and the Congo Free State became the Belgian Congo Colony, steady progress has been made towards good government. The King has visited the colony; and the interest of all the parties in it has been shown by the personal tours of their leaders. The abolition of forced labour, the improvement in the pay and quality of the officials, and the opening of successive zones to international trade have been among the measures of reform. The Congo does not yet have a very appreciable effect on the life of Belgium as a whole; but her possession of this great heritage must not be overlooked in estimating her future.

CHAPTER II

GENERAL CHARACTERISTICS OF THE COUNTRY

THE kingdom of Belgium had a population of 7,423,784 at the census of 1910, and an area of about 11,373 square miles. The area was almost exactly equal to that of the English counties of Northumberland, Cumberland, Westmoreland, Durham, and Yorkshire combined; but these counties had only four-fifths the population. The population was not far short of that of the State of Pennsylvania; but Pennsylvania covers nearly four times the Belgian area. Another comparison would be with the neighbouring country of Holland, whose area was 1275 square miles (or 11 per cent.) larger, and whose population was 1,565,509 (or 21 per cent.) smaller.

It may be noted that in Holland the population of towns with over 30,000 inhabitants was much larger, both absolutely and relatively than in Belgium; the fact being that (contrary to a common English belief) the Belgians are a more rural people than the Dutch. Their country is one in which modern travellers from abroad have been apt to visit the towns only; and like all countries with a great deal of level, it cannot be apprehended from the railway. Nevertheless its landscapes, no less than its general geographical situation in relation to Europe, have profoundly influenced the character and history of its sons. In spite of Belgium's industrial prominence, both in the Middle Ages and in the twentieth century, its agriculture is more prominent still; and possibly the success even of its industries owes not a little to the unique degree in which they are carried on by people with country homes.

The land rises by a succession of stages from the sea coast on the north-west to the low mountains of the Ardennes on the south-east. One may distinguish seven main strips of it, roughly parallel to each other. First in order, fringing the North Sea, comes a belt of sand-dunes about forty miles in length, haunted by grey mists and swept by stormy winds. Long uninhabited save by hardy fisherfolk, it has latterly developed a chain of fashionable watering-places, the chief of which is Ostend. Inland of this lies the region of *polders*, a band of reclaimed territory at or below sea-level, protected by dykes and traversed by raised causeways, treeless except for rows of poplars planted along these, but yielding rich crops from a heavy, clayey soil. Inland again we find a wide expanse of sandy soil, extending from east to west almost continuously across Belgium. The eastern tract of this, covering the north-eastern portions of the provinces of Antwerp and Limburg, is called the Campine; it consists of sterile heaths and wastes, which in recent years have been the object of systematic reclamation, and under which still more recently rich coal deposits have been proved. The western tract of sand is the celebrated plain of Flanders. Resuming our inland progress with our backs to the sea, we come next to more undulating scenery. The sand becomes loamy; finally it gives place to loam. The hills, though low, shut in the horizons nearer; and there are great forests, principally of beech, most scientifically managed. This is the typical Brabant country. As we proceed, it becomes barer; we are in an area of large farms without hedges and almost without trees. The southern portion of this is a region only second in importance to the Flemish plain, the coal-bearing district which runs across Belgium on the north side of the line of the rivers Sambre and Meuse. In modern industry (as distinct from agriculture and seaport trade) it leads the rest. Its principal industrial centres (taking them from west to east) are Mons, Charleroi, and Liége; but as we shall see, one of its notable features is the diffusion of a dense manufacturing population over a number of small towns and villages. Bordering this area and providing water-carriage for its coal and heavy goods, flows the navigable stream of the Sambre, whose line is continued from Namur onwards by the deeper and broader waters of the Meuse, sweeping to Liége through a magnificent valley walled by white limestone rocks. Beyond the river-line another and loftier zone stretches from west to east; its highest hills exceed 1000 feet. Geologically it is very varied, consisting largely of metamorphic rocks (marbles, schists, and slates) besides limestones and sandstones, and containing numerous quarries, as well as mines of iron ore, manganese, and other minerals now little exploited. This is a picturesque region with steep valleys and rocky streams recalling South Derbyshire; the surface soil is clayey, the farms large, the towns and villages smiling. Further again, still proceeding with our backs to the sea, we climb higher and reach a sterner, lonelier zone, the forest of the Ardennes. It averages nearly 1400 feet in height, though its tallest summit is only 2204; its general character is a series of lofty plateaux, whose clayey surfaces are often waterlogged marshes (*hautes fagnes*), and whose slopes are clothed in forests. Beyond them we descend finally to a smaller region, the last of the seven main tracts running from west to east, which must be traversed by the traveller who crosses Belgium from the sea. It is the limestone district of Arlon sheltered from the north by the Ardennes, and yielding an easier living to a people who alone in Belgium speak, not French or Flemish, but a Low-German dialect similar to that in the neighbouring areas of Rhenish Prussia and the Grand Duchy of Luxemburg.

Geologically, the oldest rocks in Belgium are those in the Ardennes; they are Devonian, with the earlier Cambrian formations cropping through in places. The Arlon district to the south of them is Jurassic. The districts north of them on either side of the Sambre and Meuse are Carboniferous, with a good deal of metamorphosis (limestone to marble, and shale to slate) and some eruptive intrusions of granite, etc. The northern belts of these Carboniferous rocks belong to the coal-measures; and beyond them there is a geological fault, which brings us directly to Cretaceous and Tertiary formations. The plain of Flanders is Eocene, and the Campine is Oligocene.

So much for an outline; we must now consider in more detail the two most important of these natural divisions—the great plain of Flanders, and the series of coalfields along the Sambre and Meuse. The inhabitants of the first are Flemings, and speak Flemish, a language only differing from Dutch as English does from Scots, *i.e.* they are written the same with just such differences in pronunciation and idiom as might entitle either to be termed a dialect of the other. The inhabitants of the second are called Walloons, and are classed as French-speaking; though their Walloon dialect has considerable claims to be regarded as a separate Romance language.

The Flemish plain has played a great part in the civilisation of Europe. Down to the end of the sixteenth century it was by far the most important district in the Low Countries; and to this day, despite a long series of wars and calamities, it remains a wonderful triumph of human industry over nature. The sandy soil is excessively barren. Brief neglect makes it speedily revert to desert. Yet the Flemings have made it one of the most populous, the most intensively cultivated, and the most productive areas in the entire world. To look over this plain across the *polders* from the edge of the sand-dunes is like looking over some terrestrial sea. Its flat surface stretches to the horizon, there to be lost in the characteristic blue haze whose beauty and mystery form the background of so much of the Primitive Flemish painting. In front the landscape lies in the sunshine like a carpet, diapered with countless small cultivated plots showing vivid contrasts of green and colour, and dotted thickly with whitewashed, red-roofed cottages. Planted trees abound, at intervals showing like woods, though woods of any size are rare in this busy area. Church spires point upward from every hamlet; and at close intervals lie the historic cities. Some of these, with tall, mediæval buildings rising over ancient squares, are but the ghosts of their famous selves. The old city walls are usually gone, their site often marked by modern boulevards; but the town halls and guildhalls and merchants' houses remain, and the belfry (to have which was for a mediæval town the greatest of chartered privileges, the very starting-point of collective independence) still rises in the midst, chiming the hours and quarters over quiet, pigeon-haunted streets that once surged to the sound of its tocsin. Such a city is Bruges; such were Ypres and Termonde and Malines before the European War. Dead as they were, these cities had a living influence over modern Belgium, which owes a great debt to them for its sense of beauty, its civic tradition, above all for the self-confidence which is the parent of effort. In other cases the modern revival has been effected upon the ancient sites; and the noble legacies of the Middle Ages and the Renaissance are caught up and jostled in the hurrying stream of modern progress. Such are Ghent and Antwerp; such elsewhere in Belgium are Brussels and Liége.

The coal-and-iron district along the Sambre and Meuse has not the same prestige in history as the Flemish plain. Its fortified towns, commanding one of the best military routes between France and Holland or Westphalia, have long been among the most important strategic points in Europe, the objects of numerous and famous sieges. Some of them also, especially Mons and Liége, have a tradition of industrial craftsmanship remarkably ancient and continuous. But until the nineteenth century the population and resources of the district were not comparable to those of Flanders and South Brabant. It is the modern importance of coal which has brought it to the fore.

As far back as the later Middle Ages, Liége and Mons were noted for their metalworkers and armourers, the local iron and other metallic ores being smelted by the aid of charcoal from the Ardennes forests, then more extensive than now. In the nineteenth century these industries were continued and expanded on a coal-using basis; and others, *e.g.* glass-making, were added to them. The coalfield falls into three sections; the most westerly, of which Mons is the centre, is called the Borinage; the next, lying round Charleroi, is called the Centre; the third is the coalfield of Liége. The population of all three (not merely the miners, but the ironworkers and other artisans) is unusually diffused. The largest city, Liége, has less than 200,000 inhabitants, and the great majority of the workers live in small towns and large villages which form a close network over the district. This is perhaps most noticeable round Charleroi, whose municipal area in 1912 only contained 29,452 dwellers, but whose immediate neighbourhood includes populations which, if massed in one town, would form the largest industrial town in Belgium. Collieries and ironworks do not beautify a landscape; and parts of the district (especially round Charleroi) are a sort of Black Country. On the whole, however, it is less unsightly than most areas given up to similar trades, partly owing to the picturesque lie of the land (including the fine river), partly to old and beautiful architecture, partly to the decided talent which the Belgians have for spacing and laying out buildings. All these elements are particularly to the fore in and round the city of Liége, certainly one of the most artistic of modern Europe's manufacturing centres. West of Liége, industry follows the valley of the Vesdre, a tributary stream with its source in Germany; and here the important textile town of Verviers (population in 1912, 45,964) deserves notice on account of its remoteness from the other textile centres of the country.

Politically Belgium is divided into nine provinces. This division, based on history, corresponds only roughly to the physical divisions of the country which we have just described. The provinces of West Flanders (capital Bruges) and East Flanders (capital Ghent) include the belt of sand-dunes, the strip of *polders*, and the great bulk of the Flemish plain. The latter is continued west into the province of Antwerp (capital Antwerp), where it passes into the barren heaths and pine forests of the Campine. South of the Antwerp province lies that of Brabant (strictly *South* Brabant; North Brabant being now a province of Holland), containing the capital of the kingdom, Brussels, and belonging mainly to the central region of sandy loam, rolling hills, large farms, and beech forest. The eastern extension of this region forms the dairying district of the thinly populated province of Limburg (capital Hasselt), the north and east of which is covered by the Campine. The three provinces traversed by the line of the Sambre and Meuse are Hainaut (capital Mons), Namur (capital Namur), and Liége (capital Liége). Hainaut contains the coalfields of the Borinage and the Centre, and Liége that of Liége. Each of these provinces has a share in the calcareous and quarrying region beyond the river line, but the share of Hainaut is small, and that of Namur much the largest. Namur even includes a part of the Ardennes; but the bulk of that mountainous forest area, and the whole of the sheltered limestone region which lies beyond it, are comprised in the ninth and last province, that of Belgian Luxemburg (capital Arlon). These nine provinces are important administrative units in the government of modern Belgium; but they have not, like the departments of modern France, been artificially created for the purpose. Coeval with our English counties, they have even more hold on the popular imagination and tradition, owing to the very late development of any national central government welding and transcending them.

A very important factor in the internal geography of Belgium is that of its waterways. The total length of these is about 1300 miles. The Flemish and the Walloon countries have each a principal river with a principal tributary—the Schelde and the Lys in the one case, the Meuse and the Sambre in the other. All four streams rise in France, and both the main rivers have to flow through Holland before they reach the sea. The Schelde has other navigable tributaries—the Ruppel and its feeders the Dyle, Senne, Demer, and Nethe, which drain Brabant and West Limburg, and also, draining East Flanders, the Dender and the Durme. The Meuse receives at Liége a navigable tributary, the Ourthe, from the south. In West Flanders Belgium's only other main river runs into the sea at Nieuport, the little Yser, which is

B

navigable for twenty-six miles, and has a nine-mile navigable tributary, the Yperlee. In addition to these the Flemish plain has from early times been intersected by canals, which the sandy subsoil and insignificant changes of level made it easy to excavate and construct. In the last eighty years this network has been considerably improved and extended, the most important new work being the ship canal from Zeebrugge to Bruges, intended to restore the latter city eventually to its ancient position as a great world port. That position was lost, and the city dethroned from its greatness, by the silting up in 1490 of what had been its river, the Zwyn. It is perhaps surprising that the Flemings of the Renaissance, who were then at the very top of the world's industrial achievement, contemplated the coming of this calamity for years, yet could devise no means of averting it; but political considerations (especially the jealousy of Ghent) prevented several projects from fructifying.

The watershed of the Schelde forms over 49 per cent. of the Belgian area, and that of the Meuse over 42 per cent. We have noticed that both these rivers pass to the sea through Holland. Since the Dutch became a separate nation at the end of the sixteenth century, this circumstance has operated very conspicuously to Belgium's disadvantage. It first came about during the war between Spain and the revolted Netherlands. The Spanish, under the leadership of the Prince of Parma, captured Antwerp, the great port on the Schelde, but they were unable to conquer Zeeland and what had been the Flemish strip on the left bank of the Schelde estuary; and, moreover, the Dutch wrested from them the command of the sea. The result was that Antwerp, which in 1560 had been by far the greatest port in the world, languished from 1585 to 1794 in a helpless bondage, the Dutch deliberately preventing all sea access to it in order to divert the trade to Rotterdam and Amsterdam. This " closing of the Schelde," which founded the greatness of the Dutch ports, was first stopped by the armies of the French Revolution; and the Schelde remained " open " after 1815, because Belgium was then united to Holland. But after the secession of Belgium in 1831, the Dutch revived their claim, and they persuaded the Great Powers to confirm it in a modified form by the Treaty of 1839. They were no longer to close the Schelde absolutely, but they were authorised to exact a prohibitive toll. This system was continued, to the injury of

Belgium and crippling of Antwerp, until 1863, when the Belgian Government combined with those Powers whose ships used the Schelde to buy out the Dutch toll-rights for a capital sum. The procedure followed was a copy of that adopted in 1856 to buy out the Danish toll-rights over the Sound, and in 1861 to buy out the Hanoverian toll-rights over the river Elbe. The credit of getting it applied to the Schelde's case belongs to the late Baron Lambermont, who therein showed himself a notable benefactor of his country. The freeing of the Schelde caused the commercial greatness of Antwerp to revive rapidly. In 1912 it had 312,884 inhabitants, and had become the rival of Rotterdam and Hamburg. But as a fortress (and there was a very important rôle assigned to it as a fortress—that of providing a last refuge on Belgian soil for the Government of an invaded Belgium) it was, and still is, gravely weakened by the Dutch ownership of the Schelde estuary. The waters of this estuary, flowing between Dutch banks on either side, are themselves in law part of the actual territory of Holland. Antwerp therefore can be neither attacked nor relieved from the sea without a violation of Dutch neutrality; and it was this fact which in 1914 compelled the

Belgian Army and Government to evacuate it.

The grievance regarding the Meuse is purely commercial; but it is not insignificant. This fine river is the waterway for the coal-and-iron district of Belgium; and being canalised by the Belgians down to Visé, where it leaves their territory, is navigated by inland steamers. It cannot, however, be navigated to the sea, because the Dutch, though they navigate it from the mouth up to Venlo, refuse to canalise the remaining strip from Venlo to Visé. There are no rapids or other great obstacles to prevent this work being done; and if it were done, Liége would become a great seaport, shipping its heavy export manufactures (guns, locomotives, and motor-cars) direct. But that is precisely what the Dutch, with their inveterate commercial jealousy of the Belgian seaports, do not appear to desire.

What may be termed the " external geography " of Belgium (that is, its situation in regard to the other countries of the world), has more than any other factor shaped its destiny. It is for trade purposes the natural meeting-ground of the West European nations; unfortunately it has for the same reasons been again and again their battle-ground. Lying between England, France, Germany, and Holland, it has good water communications with each. Though not quite so near the English coast as a corner of France is, it has the great advantage of exactly fronting the mouth of the Thames. With France it is connected by the upper courses of the Lys, Schelde, Sambre, and Meuse, the last named being navigable for barge traffic right away up into Lorraine. With Germany its connection is less direct; the outlet of the Rhine, of course, is through Holland, and not through Belgium at all; but there are canal communications with Westphalia, and the proximity of the Lower Rhine towns has always been an influence in Belgian life. The inhabitants of this middle land, between some of the principal French and German districts and London, were in the Mediæval and Renaissance periods enabled to make the very most of their situation through the excellence of their internal waterways and the sheltered positions of their ports. In the days of piracy a harbour on the coast itself was not the best place for trade. Towns like the Cinque Ports in Kent, or Calais and Dunkirk on the Franco-Flemish seaboard, were of naval and military importance rather than commercial. Even Antwerp was for many centuries little but a fortress guarding the head of the Schelde estuary, the chief port of the river being far higher up, at Ghent, where the Lys joins it. When the obsolescence of piracy and the deeper draught of vessels modified these conditions, Antwerp was there, ready to benefit by the change. In the last eighty years Belgium has been similarly helped by its railway system, thanks to the commercial foresight of its first king. Fares and freights on the Belgian State Railways are the lowest in Europe; and they are so well linked up that for many years Brussels has enjoyed express communication with Paris, Frankfort, Vienna, Berlin, and Holland, as well as with Italy via Bâle, and with London via Ostend and Dover. The country has thus come to form at the heart of the most industrial and commercial region of the Old World a centre and meeting-point not only for trade and finance, but for art, for literature, for ideas, in a word, for civilisation; and stimulated by constant contact with foreign example, its own effort both in manufacture, in agriculture, and in the finer arts of life has been able to reach a high level.

CHAPTER III

GENERAL CHARACTERISTICS OF THE PEOPLE

As might be expected from their geographical position, the racial origins of the Belgian people are extremely mixed; and this is reflected in their physical appearance. Pure ethnic types are rare. Nevertheless there are two, which may be easily distinguished above the rest as contributing the main elements to the various hybrid varieties. One is the blonde, long-skulled type of North Germany, which is on the whole the dominant type in Holland. The other is the short, dark, short-skulled type of South Germany and Eastern France. If for brevity we call these by the conventional (though unsatisfactory) names " Teutonic " and " Alpine," we may say that throughout Walloon Belgium the Alpine type dominates, often in comparative purity; and the same type counts for a great deal in the Flemish provinces, though

40

here it is much overlaid by the Teutonic. The latter is only dominant in the sand-dune belt and parts of the *polder* region; and even there is seldom seen at all pure. The paintings of the early Flemish and Brabant masters show the Alpine type to have been dominant in the great Belgian cities as early as the Burgundian epoch.

While it has often been loosely said that the English and the Belgians are physically much alike, this is only true of individuals. It may be, for instance, that a bargee from the Medway and a bargee from Ostend are indistinguishable. But in the first place both are likely to be dominated by a common Teutonic type, which is not dominant in either country taken as a whole; and in the second place the population of Kent (as that of several other English counties) was very appreciably affected by the enormous immigration of Flemish Protestant refugees in the sixteenth century. Apart from such immigrations the Alpine type, usually dominant in Belgium, is scarcely found in the British Isles, being replaced by varieties of the so-called Iberian type; which, though also short and dark, is long skulled. Consequently most Belgians appear to a British eye rather noticeably broad in the head and flat in the face,

B 2

with a marked fullness at the temples; while British faces by contrast seem narrow and projecting, with hollow temples and deeper-set eyes. The dominance of the Alpine type in Belgium gives the nation a very low average stature (in this they are veritably *petits Belges*); and the types mainly responsible for the tallest men and women in the British Isles—the Scandinavian immigrants of the Viking period, and the blonde, rather short-skulled, red-haired type so conspicuous in some of our " Celtic " regions—hardly occur along the Schelde and the Meuse. But though short, the ordinary Belgian workman is broad and extremely muscular; and he has had for centuries, whether Fleming or Walloon, whether in agriculture or industry, a reputation for hard work and stamina second to none in Europe.

Attempts to disentangle component racial types must not lead us to forget that the Belgian nation in all its provinces is essentially an outcome of hybridisation and selection; and has developed, like other notable hybrid nations, distinctive stocks of its own of special value. The people who built up the great civilisations of Flanders and Brabant in the Middle Ages were not an ordinary breed; they evinced abilities and character of a very exceptional kind. From 1555 to 1815 the conditions which historic fortune imposed on their existence were such as would have stamped a weaker folk out; and they were wholly precluded from any sort of national brilliance. But when the yoke was at last lifted off in the nineteenth century, their old qualities speedily blossomed afresh. Only a people with a strong and individual heritage of ability passing from ancestors to descendants could have renewed across such an interval the features of its former glory.

Most of this heritage was fixed early in history. Conquest and immigration have added subsequent outside elements to the original (say, before the year 1000) interchange and consolidation of types; though fewer than is often supposed. Some of the attempts to trace them appear decidedly fanciful; e. g. the common suggestion that a peculiar and elegant carriage to be noticed sometimes among the women is " Andalusian " and shows descent from the occupying Spaniards of the sixteenth and seventeenth centuries. The feature in question seems far more naturally explained by the peasant women's habit of carrying burdens on their heads; for the definite and measurable characteristics of the Iberian type appear to be rare in Belgium; and in point of fact most of the occupying "Spanish" troops were Walloons. In quite recent times the foreigners resident in Belgium have become rather numerous in proportion to population. The census of 1910 showed 254,547 of them, including 80,765 French, 57,010 Germans, 70,950 Dutch, and only 6974 English. There was a considerable colony of Russian Jews at Antwerp; but elsewhere the Jewish elements in Belgium are numerically small. The tendency since the development of railways has been for Belgians of every district to form connections with those of every other district, and to consolidate a common national type. But the growth of the indigenous population, though rapid, has not prevented a parallel tendency for foreigners to be drawn in. It is largely a matter of industrial and commercial specialisation; for Belgium, while importing some kinds of foreign labour, exports other kinds of her own. At various seasons of the year tens of thousands of her sons have been in the habit of working temporarily in neighbouring countries, particularly in France at the sugar-beet harvest.

In loose parlance the Flemings and Walloons are often spoken of as the two "races" of

Belgium; but the dividing line between them is not ethnical. It is primarily linguistic; and there are also some differences of temper and tradition, specialised by historical segregation. The Walloons are a people inhabiting country for the most part semi-mountainous and by nature picturesque. Man has not composed its beauties, though he has latterly often disfigured them by slag-heaps; and its wealth in old days was rather that of forest, pastures, and quarries than that of tilled land. The ancestors of its present population belonged largely to what are called backward classes—foresters, hunters, charcoal-burners, shepherds, mountain crofters, and similar hardy dwellers on the outskirts of civilisation. Many were soldiers of fortune; for during two centuries it was the recruiting ground of the best mercenaries in Europe. Its chief traditional industries were quarrying, smiths' work, and the manufacture of arms; and upon these coal-mining, steel-smelting, and engineering have been grafted in modern times. In direct contrast, the Flemings are the natives of a featureless plain, on which the unremitting human labour of eleven centuries has visibly conferred every element of beauty or wealth that it possesses. By the patient tillage to which every spare acre is subjected, the barren Flemish sand was taught to yield two crops, where more favoured regions yield only one; by patient laying of brick upon brick, the belfries of town halls and the spires of cathedrals were raised to heaven to afford the points of outlook and rallying which no natural elevations afforded. The same patient spirit reared the skilled fortifications which provided defences in the naturally defenceless plain; built up behind them for the first time in history a manufacturing wealth based on foreign trade at both ends—alike on the import of raw materials and on the export of finished goods; and, by the slow, stubborn accumulation of charters and precedents wrung from reluctant feudal lords, established for their burghers the privileged right to live their lives in their own way. The Fleming is the heir to the oldest and most sorely tried of modern civilisations, except the Italian; there is bred in his bone a conservative tenacity, a rooted instinct of loyalty to the religion and traditions of the past, a plodding, pondering habit of mind, and the sedulous detailed industry of the intensive cultivator and the handicraftsman. The Walloon on the other hand represents a hastier and perhaps bolder (certainly more martial) type, which has passed by a leap from the lowest to the highest rung of the modern industrial ladder; he lives without rest in a world of innovation, in which he has accomplished great things, but is in travail for the accomplishment of greater; he is a revolutionary, a transformer, at best a creator. In art the deepest characteristics of the Flemings have never been more faithfully expressed than by the fifteenth-century Flemish painters—with their contemplative and mystical inspiration, their close observance of prescription and ritual, their patient and masterly drawing, their solid and sumptuous colour, and the meticulous detail which renders every hair on a flesh surface and cannot be fully appreciated without a magnifying lens. The Walloons might, for contrast, be illustrated by their great modern sculptor, Constantin Meunier; the unity and life of whose mightiest conceptions seem as if they were projected into the bronze or stone by a single effort of the demiurgic mind.

These differences reflect themselves in politics. The Walloons tend to be Liberals or Socialists, and strongly anti-clerical; while the Flemish-speaking population supplies most of the voters for the Catholic party, which has been in power in the Belgian Parliament without interruption since 1884. Such a coincidence between a linguistic division and the divisions of party and creed is, to say the least of it, not fortunate; and it has led in recent years to a regrettable sharpening of the language conflict. This conflict was first shaped in the middle of the nineteenth century by the movement of the *flamingants*, or Flemishisers. The original motive of *flamingantisme* was defence. Its leaders found the old Flemish tongue in a position of inferiority and in danger of dying out of all but working-class use. The average French-speaking Belgian was not unwilling that it should. French had been the language of the upper classes in Flanders since the Middle Ages; and as a widely known European language, possessing a great literature and also great commercial utility, it had some obvious advantages over a particularist speech, which outside North Belgium could only be understood in Holland and was there regarded as bad Dutch. Against this the *flamingants* insisted that a people's maternal language is a part of its very soul, to be neglected or lost at its peril, and that Flemish was the maternal language of more than half Belgium. Encouraged by the blossoming of a decidedly remarkable Flemish literature, they claimed the full equality of the languages for official and educational uses; and this, if a foreigner may venture a controversial opinion, they seem in substance to have gained. But within the twentieth century they developed a new discontent with their position. In part, perhaps, this was due to the growing evidence that Flemish needed much more than a fair field and no favour if it was to overcome its natural handicaps in the race with French. But in part it was certainly a by-product of the anti-French feeling revived in Catholic Flanders by the victories of anti-clericalism in France and the separation of Church and State there. Dislike of the French is a very old Flemish instinct. In nearly all the wars in Flanders, from the battle of Cassel in 1071 to that of Waterloo in 1815, the French were the invaders; and in the centuries of conflict between the Flemish city communes and feudalism, French armies were always the mainstay of the latter. The later *flamingant* movement rekindled these memories, took on a decidedly aggressive aspect, and developed what had been a language question into a conflict of religious, political, and even international importance.

How far German influences were responsible for fanning *flamingantisme* to excess it is impossible to say. The leading *flamingants* were not conscious Germanisers. But German sympathy with the extension of Flemish and diminution of French was natural; and the German Government must have departed from its usual practice if it did not employ agents to foster such a process. At all events the later extravagances, if we may use the word, of the *flamingant* agitation appear to have coincided in date with the growth of definite German designs against Belgian independence.

Foreign observers have perhaps been prone to overrate the seriousness of the schism between Flemings and Walloons. In the first place the two populations are very evenly matched in number, and neither has much chance of absorbing the other. The Flemish-speaking population in 1910 was 3,229,314, the French-speaking 2,908,327, and the bilingual 923,835. These figures are not beyond challenge, and that for bilinguals is probably much too low. A man will commonly return himself French-speaking or Flemish-speaking, according to the language in which he was brought up, even though for business purposes he has a working knowledge of the other. But the distinction between maternal languages remains, and its boundaries do not greatly alter. Secondly, the two languages have each their geographical spheres of influence; it is not a question of a ruling race and a subject race jostling each other in fierce competition all over a disputed country. Thirdly, with all their differences the Flemings and Walloons are conscious of a common destiny. They have lived together under a single government for nearly five centuries (excepting the people of Liége, who, however, are particularly " Belgian " in sentiment); and they much prefer each other's partnership in independence to a dependent association with anybody else. The French-speaking Walloons have no desire to be annexed by France; and the Flemings, though their language is quasi-identical with Dutch, are extremely averse to being absorbed in the Dutch people. The German invasion of 1914–1915, uniting all Belgians without distinction of race or party in a common national feeling against the ruthless aggressor, may very possibly leave behind it a spirit of greater tolerance and mutual accommodation between the champions of the two languages; when what is not on its intrinsic merits a really difficult problem may perhaps receive a settlement agreeable to all.

The divergence between the Flemings and

the Dutch deserves careful notice. Before
the disastrous reign of its first Spanish ruler,
Philip II (1555–1598), Flanders was a very
much more important country than Holland,
and its cities altogether larger and richer.
The result of the struggles against Philip II
was that Holland obtained its independence
and was carried by the impetus of its emanci-
pation into the position of a Great Power;
while Belgium, devastated and depopulated
by the Duke of Alva, remained under the
Spanish dominion, and was prevented from
recovering its economic prosperity by the
action of the Dutch in closing the Schelde.
The commercial jealousy, which for several
centuries impelled the Dutch thus deliberately to keep Belgium poor, was not calculated
to endear them to their victims; and the
incidents of the brief period (1815–1830)
when the Dutch and Belgian peoples were
united under the Dutch Crown only deepened
the antipathy. It rests, however, not only
on accidents of history, but on strong contrasts of habit and taste. We have already
compared the relation of the Dutch and Flemish languages to that between Scots and
English; and the parallel might be pursued
further in the comparison of their national
characters. The Dutch, like the Scots, are

Calvinists; the Flemings clung to Catholicism, as the English did to Prelacy. The traditional Dutchman (the type has no doubt been blurred by modernity) is something of a Puritan, affecting black clothes and bare unornamented interiors; the Fleming is a great lover of feasting and joviality, of sensuous colours and sumptuous fabrics and florid magnificence in architecture. The Flemish delight in pomp and ritual, and the Flemish mysticism, are alien to the Dutch, who are at once less gross and less spiritual. Dutch life strikes a Fleming as drab and austere; Flemish life strikes a Dutchman as untidy and lax and superstitious. Naturally a hard people, the Dutch have become, perhaps, over-engrossed in trading gains; their cities live by buying and selling the work of other men's hands, which seldom does more than pass through their own. Flanders has less of the purely mercantile and more of the industrial temperament; she is more constructive, less skinflint, more idealist. The contrast may be worked out even to the national beverages. The Dutch, like the Scots, are spirit drinkers; it was they who invented gin. The Flemings, like the English, drink beer. Flemish ales have been famous since the thirteenth century, and were the first to obtain a considerable reputation outside their own borders. It is true that gin drinking has latterly made a singularly maleficent progress in Belgium among the working classes; but the ravages of this fiery spirit, which have come to be regarded by thoughtful Belgians as one of the chief dangers to their national physique and character, are the more marked precisely because the population have no hereditary familiarity with it.

All such differences could have been bridged, and the Dutch and Flemings united, as the English and Scots were, had the course of history favoured it. In that case the Belgian and Dutch Netherlands, consolidated as a single state, would have formed a Great Power, whose territory none of its neighbours could violate lightly. This was the conception of the Burgundian Dukes; the conception of William the Silent; and, in the nineteenth century, the conception of the Duke of Wellington, who was the main author of the kingdom of the United Netherlands set up by the Congress of Vienna. The circumstances under which that last experiment broke up render it unlikely that it will ever be repeated. Even the fine National Anthem of modern Belgium, the " Brabançonne," is an expression of anti-Dutch feeling, and a perpetual reminder of the wrongs suffered by Belgium from the Dutch ruling house. Nothing but the flood of some very destructive and transforming revolution, which would have to sweep over the two countries at the same time, can be conceived as capable of submerging such solidly established barriers.

An important factor in the temperament of any people at a given time is the rate of growth of the population. Where this is slow, the inhabitants of a country can with little effort maintain their traditional standards of comfort; where it stagnates or declines, effort is apt to stagnate or decline also. Where on the other hand population increases rapidly, there results almost inevitably a spirit of uneasiness and hustle, seeking new outlets for energy and new reapportionments of wealth. In such a ferment it is that the great movements of social or imperial or religious idealism tend to be born. Belgium since 1830 has nearly always shown a rapid growth of population. In the thirty years between the censuses of 1880 and 1910 the increase was over 34 per cent. In the United Kingdom the corresponding census period (1881–1911) shows an increase of 28 per cent.; in France (1881–1911) it was 5 per cent.; in the German Empire (1880–1910) it was 43 per cent. Belgium, therefore, though much behind the phenomenal growth of Germany, was well ahead of its two great western neighbours; and in estimating the effect of such growth we must not forget that it is the most thickly populated state in Europe, and, save in the Campine, has very few empty spaces to fill up. The increase does not result from a high birth-rate; for though births in Catholic Flanders are well maintained, in the Walloon provinces they are sinking under French influences towards the French level. It is due to the combination of a moderate birth-rate (practically the same as the English) with a low death-rate and an almost complete absence of permanent emigration.

Personal habits play an important and often underestimated part in the life of a nation, especially those traditional habits of housewifery, cooking, clothing, etc., which among the less sophisticated masses transmit from generation to generation the painfully accumulated hoard of race-experience, and if lost are so difficult to replace by any formal instruction or book learning. Belgium suffered incalculably, and had all its standards of life lowered by its miseries during the long period when it was the " cockpit of Europe." But it has never in modern times undergone such a violent breach in the continuity of its popular habits as was inflicted on Great Britain by the abruptness and unforeseenness of her Industrial Revolution, on France (to a less extent) by her Political Revolution and the Napoleonic Wars, and on nations like latter-day America by the wholesale immixture of foreign populations from a dozen different national soils. The Belgians have, for instance, what the English have not, a skilled system of popular cookery traditional throughout the nation, diffused upwards from the immemorial experience of the peasantry. For the palate of the international epicure it is not to be mentioned with the handiwork of French or Italian *chefs ;* but as providing all the poorer classes with a popular dietary suited to the climate, nutritious, digestible, mainly home-grown, and remarkably cheap, it is a real asset for national efficiency. So with clothing; from his cheap, warm, dry wooden shoes (the ordinary French *sabots*) upwards, the Belgian workman wears what is inexpensive but practical and suitable to his occupation, instead of (as so largely English and American workmen do) what is dear and unsuitable; and moreover his wife knows how to mend and darn and use pieces. Of course the modern tendency, whereby the clerk tries to dress like a rich man, and the workman like a clerk, and the great majority of people to spend an ever-growing part of their income on clothing necessarily bad of its kind and undesigned for their needs, does not leave Belgium entirely untouched; but it encounters there a resistance from the better tradition, which it does not encounter in countries whose traditions have been lost. One has only to compare the get-up of, let us say, a porter in the great Brussels markets with that of a similar porter in a London or Manchester market, in order to appreciate the Belgian's advantage in this respect: an advantage the more worthy of note because the actual money takings of the English porter would be considerably higher.

The experience which lies behind Belgian habits is mainly that of rural life, which (though there are many systems of farming, according to the varieties of soil and practice in the various districts, and small holdings are by no means a uniform or universal feature) may be broadly termed peasant life. In some areas, especially among the small cultivators of East and West Flanders, this life goes with a narrow range of ideas and an extreme conservatism in religion and politics. But even there the peasantry are not unprogressive all round; they are constantly adopting the newest agricultural methods suited to their particular farming. There are, too, many features which the English observer must beware of condemning simply because they are unfamiliar, or because in the different conditions of his own country they would entail different consequences. Such a feature is the field work of women. It must by no means be regarded as a mere symptom of poverty or sex-oppression. A Belgian peasant who works for himself and whose wife and daughters work with him out-of-doors at the heaviest tasks may be richer in money (as well as far better housed, better fed, and better clothed) than the English labourer who works for a farmer at twelve or fifteen shillings a week, and whose indoor anæmic wife, with her diet of tea and white bread and patent medicines, would be ashamed to be seen engaged in any but the lightest of open-air work. Nor can the Belgian peasant women with their vigorous self-assertion, powerful physique, and capable housewifery be regarded as more downtrodden than their sisters in English villages. The traditional peasant existence has its animal, and even

brutal aspects; but it provides better than
its British counterparts for the physical
vigour of both sexes, a vigour which cannot
but tell for the survival and success of the
people as a whole.

Town life in Belgium has also a long history
and tradition behind it. Of its political
characteristics we will speak elsewhere. Here
we will notice how much less sharp than in
England is the breach between country and
town habits. Owing to the constriction of
the largest Belgian towns by fortifications,
the urban working class has not escaped the
great evil of lofty tenement buildings, from
which the English cities almost alone in
Europe are relatively free. But the policy
long pursued by the Government on the State
Railways has been remarkably effective in
preventing Belgian urban life from being
swamped by the townward rush of modernity.
There is no land in the world where so large
a proportion of the workers in the towns have
their homes in the country. Consequently
both the size and the rate of growth of the
great cities have remained manageable. It
is impossible to find, as in England, square
miles of smoky, mean streets, where scarcely
anything green lives and Nature means nothing to the children. Town planning has

not been developed to German lengths; but very effective work has been done, especially at the capital; and it is impossible to deny some great æsthetic merits to the modern as well as the ancient portions of the Belgian cities. Nor do the working class, transplanted from peasant life to urban, part with their practical domestic traditions. A good instance is the " Flemish stove," an urban contrivance now common in the country also, which corresponds in the working-class kitchen living-room to the miniature cooking-range which a similar room in England usually has built into its wall. In proportion to the fuel consumed, such a stove yields very considerably more heat both for cooking and for warming the room than the range built into the wall does, while its easier accessibility for cooking saves the housewife a great deal of labour. Moreover, it is practically smokeless, and contributes powerfully to the almost complete freedom of the Belgian towns from domestic smoke.

Although the factors which we have just described have enabled the Belgian working classes to live considerably better on their low wages than English workmen could do, it remains unfortunately the case that these are the lowest in West Europe, and far too

low, in many instances, for any efficient or
worthy life to be lived. This is true both of
industry and agriculture, and is the darkest
feature of the country's material development.
If one wished to see the Belgian peasant and
domestic tradition at its worst, one would
perhaps do so in the case of sweated home
industries. The habits of the peasant house-
hold lead into these by a natural transition.
They are numerous in Belgium; and there,
as elsewhere, the weight of the direst poverty
and exploitation hangs over them. Nothing
in the whole country is more squalid and degraded than the conditions of certain moderate-
sized and obscure towns, chiefly in Flanders,
which are given up to such industries and are
practically unrelieved slums, islanded in the
country-side, from whose squeezed-out or
deluded workers they recruit their victims.

It is curious that with all the heritage of
civilised tradition, on which we have just laid
stress, the Belgians are conspicuously lacking
on one side, in which tradition might have
been expected to tell. Their warmest foreign
sympathisers can hardly claim for them with
candour that as a people they have attractive
manners. No doubt their old nobility is as
cultivated as any other; and the contact
with public duties and responsibilities, which

under a constitutional monarchy it has been able to preserve, distinguishes it rather favourably from the French, just as its lack of unpopular privileges distinguishes it from the English. The intellectual and higher professional class have also a cosmopolitan polish. But it is not by such thin upper strata that one samples a nation's manners; one must judge by its masses—its labourers and peasants, its farmers and shopkeepers, its tram conductors and railway porters and policemen. Tested in this way, there are some European peoples—the Italians and the Irish, for instance, and on the whole the French —who seem endowed with a natural friendliness and unstudied courtesy. There are others —for example, the Scots of the east coast and the Scandinavians, and on the whole the Dutch—who make up for a lack of affability by that simplicity, sincerity, and restraint of impulse which is another aspect of good breeding. The Belgians scarcely rank high in either category. They are rather a mulish, lumpish people, slow to help the stranger, suspicious, surly, disobliging, exacting, and ungrateful. No doubt these qualities (some of which a good many foreigners will observe in Lancashire and Yorkshire no less than in Flanders and Brabant) go along with, and are perhaps inherent in a valuable doggedness and strength of will. The peoples with most personal grace and charm are not always those that achieve the most solid performances, and the Belgians can safely take their stand on the latter before the bar of history. Nevertheless their disagreeable features have delayed the recognition of their merits, and made possible the blindness of that army of tourists who have roamed the Belgian towns and admired their ancient monuments without in the least realising that the living men around them were genuine descendants of their authors, and had in their day and generation toiled not less honourably along the higher paths of human endeavour.

CHAPTER IV

THE HISTORIC GLORIES OF BELGIUM

THE Belgium with which we are concerned came into being for the first time as a distinct independent state in 1830. But that is very far from being the first page in its history. Its nine provinces had in 1815 been assigned by the Congress of Vienna to the new Dutch monarchy, which the Congress created; and during the years 1815–1830 had formed part of a United Kingdom of the Netherlands. Previous to that they had from 1795 belonged first to Revolutionary and then to Napoleonic France. During the whole of these thirty-five years preceding their independence they had, though subject, been strengthening their sense of a common nationality.

For eight of the nine provinces this sense had long existed. The ninth was Liége, which till 1795 was an ecclesiastical state by itself, the domain for nine centuries of a line of bishops who were princes of the Holy Roman

C

Empire. The other provinces had always been under the rule of a common sovereign since they were first united under the Dukes of Burgundy in the middle of the fifteenth century. They passed from the House of Burgundy to the House of Austria in 1482; and on the abdication of the great Emperor Charles V in 1555, they passed together with what is now Holland to the rule of the Spanish monarchy. The revolt against Spain, which broke out thirteen years later, ended in the establishment of Holland as an independent state. The eight provinces which we are considering (together with some territories since annexed by France and Holland) were those left in Spanish hands; and they thus for the first time formed a political entity by themselves, being known in contradistinction to Holland as the " Spanish Netherlands." In 1713 they passed by the Treaty of Utrecht to Austria; and until annexed by France in 1795, were known as the " Austrian Netherlands."

It was during this last period that the term " Belgians " first began to be popularly applied to the people; though it had been used in Latin documents to describe the people of the Low Countries as far back as the Middle Ages. Its origin, of course, is the name " Belgæ," given by the Romans to the inhabitants of the country in Cæsar's time. Its modern use, both in Latin documents and in the stilted French and English poetic language of the period 1650–1750, was to signify the Dutch scarcely less than the Belgians. As a distinctive term for the people, excluding the Dutch, the French noun " Belges " had become general by the time of the Brabant Revolution (1789), but its adjectival form was then " Belgique."

Thus we see that (leaving on one side the case of Liége) the Belgian provinces have (1) been under a common sovereign since before the time of the English Wars of the Roses; (2) formed a territory distinct from the neighbouring territories since the time of the Armada. Let us add that before the disastrous period of Spanish rule they had never since Frankish times been subject in the modern sense to foreigners. The Dukes of Burgundy, who first united them, were not conquering invaders, but the heirs of indigenous families, who gradually brought into their single family the dukedoms and countships of the various provinces. The greatest of them, Philip the Good, made Bruges and Ghent his principal capitals. Nor did the Habsburgs at first rule as foreigners. The

Emperor Charles V, whose dominions included Austria, Spain, and the Americas, besides the Low Countries, was always most at home in these last. He was born at Ghent, and he chose Brussels as the scene of his abdication ceremony. Belgium supplied him with the bulk of his wealth, and also with some of his best soldiers. The first ruler who treated the people of the Low Countries as the subordinate subjects of a foreign power was Philip II of Spain. But from the time of his accession they were never really treated otherwise till 1830.

The name and fame of the Belgian provinces goes back far earlier than their union under Philip the Good. The Carlovingian founders of the Holy Roman Empire were natives of the province of Liége. Pepin, the first Mayor of the Palace, was born there at Landen, and his grandson, the father of Charles Martel, at Herstal (where in recent times has stood one of the principal Liége forts). The empire consolidated by Charles Martel and Charlemagne, essentially a union of France and West Germany, found its natural centre in South Belgium and the adjoining district of Aix-la-Chapelle. When this broke up and was divided in three by Charlemagne's grandsons, Flanders, though its speech was Germanic,

went with the Western third (the prototype
of modern France); while the rest of Belgium,
though Latin-speaking, went with the middle
third, called Lotharingia (Lorraine), which
included the whole of the country between the
rivers Rhine, Moselle, Meuse, and Schelde.
In the two stormy centuries which followed
this break-up, were established the great
feudal positions of the Count of Flanders,
the Count of Hainaut, the Duke of Brabant,
and the Marquis of Antwerp. The Duchy of
Limburg, the Countdom of Luxemburg, and
the Countdom of Namur were carved out of
the original Duchy of Brabant, but are early
and famous nevertheless. These feudal divisions, with some clipping of their outer
frontiers, but little change where they adjoin
each other, form (with the addition of the
Prince-Bishopric of Liége) the Belgian provinces of to-day. The Bishop of Liége became
a great temporal potentate in the tenth
century, and a prince of the Holy Roman
Empire at the beginning of the eleventh.

The feudal framework of Duchies, Countdoms, and Prince-Bishopric, has had a deep
historic influence on the Belgian people. To
the present day all the principal provinces
have a character and tradition of their own,
matched and enhanced by a much more dis-

tinctive counterpart in written history than
is the case even with the English counties.
The chivalry of the Low Countries (and until
the rising against Spain at the end of the
sixteenth century "the Low Countries"
chiefly meant Belgium, Holland being relatively quite unimportant) was among the
most splendid in Europe; and it took a
prominent part in the principal military
enterprises of the Middle Ages, e. g. the
Crusades and the battles of the Hundred
Years War. Godfrey of Bouillon, a Walloon,
Marquis of Antwerp, was the first knight to
scale the walls of Rome, when the Emperor
Henry IV warred against Pope Gregory VII;
he was also, together with Robert, Count of
Flanders, the foremost military leader in the
First Crusade, and became the first King
of Jerusalem. Counts of Flanders were prominent in several subsequent Crusades, the
most notable being Baldwin IX (who was also
Count of Hainaut), who led the Fifth Crusade,
captured and sacked Constantinople, and was
in 1204 crowned in St. Sophia as Emperor of
the East. The Belgian dynasties at Jerusalem
and Constantinople undoubtedly widened the
trade connections of Flanders; in particular
the relations established with Venice in the
course of the Fifth Crusade must have helped

to show the Flemings the pathways to commercial wealth, along which they were shortly to outdistance Venice herself. It is from the time of that Crusade that the rapid expansion of the great cities of Flanders and Brabant dates. The effect of all the Crusades was to occupy and kill off the feudal nobles and their military caste, and so leave the urban middle classes freer for development. Moreover, they caused the nobility to need money on quite a new scale; and this they obtained from the towns in return for charters and concessions.

The history of the Belgian cities is the most brilliant part of Belgian history before 1830. It is inseparable from the chief special contributions, which the country has made to the civilisation of Europe; and save for the parallel development of the Italian cities, and the much weaker and less forward growth of the German free towns, it is unique. Its distinctive features began to be first visible in Flanders. That region (as we showed in the second chapter) is by nature sterile; and its chief assets in the Dark Ages were its ports, its waterways, and the fact that it lay just opposite the mouth of the Thames. After its Count Baldwin I, called Iron-Arm, had repelled the Northmen towards the end of the ninth century, his son Baldwin II (son-in-

law of our Alfred the Great) fortified the four
cities of Bruges, Ghent, Courtrai, and Ypres,
which ever since have been the most famous
places in Flanders proper. Thereafter, the
Flemings began to concentrate their attention
on shipping, cloth manufacture, and trade
with England. The cloth markets appear to
have been established in the chief towns about
the year 960. England, which very early was
(as it still is) the principal sheep-growing
country in Europe, supplied the raw wool.
At the same time Flanders itself grew (as it
still does) a great deal of flax for linen; in
treating which the water of the river Lys has
always had a peculiar efficacy. In 1066 the
then Count of Flanders, Baldwin V, who was
father-in-law to William the Conqueror, took
a very active part in the conquest of England.
Flemish ships conveyed a large proportion
of the invaders to Pevensey; Flemish knights
won by their swords some of the principal
English fiefs in the Conqueror's disposal; and
for many centuries Flemish clerks and officials
came to play a regular, if often unpopular,
part in most English administrations. Leaders
of popular risings in England seem to have
been as anxious to " kill all the Flemings "
as to " kill all the lawyers." Thus in the
fourteenth century Chaucer tells us in his

Nun Priest's Tale of the shouting of " Jacke Strawe and his meynee, *whan that they wolden any Fleming kille.*"

Baldwin V's son, Baldwin VI, married Richilde, the heiress of Hainaut, thus effecting an important union of provinces; and it was he who in 1068 conferred on the town of Grammont the first of the Flemish town charters. His widow, Richilde, subsequently oppressed the Flemish cities with the aid of the French king, still her feudal superior; but Ypres, Courtrai, and Tournai rose against her, and under the command of her husband's brother, Robert of Flanders, heavily defeated her in the two days' battle of Cassel Hill (1071), though she had the full military support of the King of France. This famous battle, in which for the first time in mediæval Europe a great feudal army of knights and men-at-arms was beaten by burgher levies, raised the prestige of the Flemish cities to a new point; and it was then that the Crusades supervened, as we have seen, to enrich them and to weaken their feudal over-lords.

From the twelfth to the sixteenth centuries the story of the Belgian towns is one of civic life, wealth, and industry, struggling to maintain itself against a military environment. The brunt of the struggle fell upon Flanders.

C 2

The chief cities of Brabant, Louvain and Brussels, were on a smaller scale; they owed more to their feudal rulers, the very enlightened dynasty of the Dukes of Brabant, and contented themselves more easily with being those rulers' capitals. The cities of Walloon Belgium were prevented from rivalling Flanders by their remoteness from the sea; and though those of Hainaut were often involved in the same conflicts as the Flemish through the inter-marriage of the dynasties of the two Countdoms, those of Liége revolved in an orbit of their own under the Prince-Bishops, and enjoyed from the eleventh to the fifteenth centuries an unusual measure of peace and order, thanks to the celebrated " tribunal of peace " established by the Bishops in Liége Cathedral. But whereas the rest of Belgium was part of the Holy Roman Empire, Flanders was still a fief of France. Indeed, when the great French King, Philip Augustus, began to consolidate the French monarchy at the opening of the thirteenth century, the Count of Flanders was the most formidable vassal with whom he had to deal. Philip Augustus's efforts to destroy Flemish independence were the first of a long series made by the French kings, efforts in direct conflict with the rising spirit and power of the Flemish burghers.

The struggle was apt to be fought out as between rival claimants to the Countdom, one claimant being supported by the French king in consideration of his advancing French sovereignty, the other by the burghers of the towns in consideration of his extending their town privileges. From an early stage the Flemish patriots sought English alliances against France. The first was with our King John against Philip Augustus, and it came to a disastrous end at the battle of Bouvines (1214)—one of the most decisive battles in history, since it may be said in France to have founded the unity of the French nation, and in England to have directly brought about the concession of Magna Charta. It threw Flanders under French sovereignty for nearly a century; though in that period civil war and French invasions occurred more than once. But in 1296 the then Count put himself at the head of the Flemish popular party, and definitely threw off the French yoke, contracting an alliance (the League of Grammont) with Edward I of England, the Emperor, and the Duke of Brabant. Again the French were victorious; the Count's great allies were bought off by the French King, Philip the Fair; and by 1300 Flanders was completely subdued. In 1301, the bulk of the Flemish nobles and knights (excepting the "Leliaerts," or French faction) being in prison, Philip the Fair visited Bruges and Ghent as a conqueror, imposed alteration on their civic constitutions, and returned, leaving an oppressive French Lieutenant-General behind him. But the proud and turbulent artisans of the rich Flemish cities were in no mind to be trampled on like the French serfs. A remarkable insurrection broke out at Bruges under Pieter de Coninc, a weaver, and Jan Breydel, a butcher. At first the French made headway against it; but then Coninc and Breydel re-entered Bruges, and in the celebrated "Mattins of Bruges" (May 1302) the entire French garrison was cut to pieces by the infuriated artisans. Philip the Fair's reply was to dispatch within two months a magnificent army, including all the finest chivalry of France, against the insurgents. The patriot burghers could only meet this menace with an army half its size, nearly destitute of cavalry, and composed principally of artisans armed with pikes. But the battle of Courtrai, which followed, proved the Bannockburn of Flanders. There have been few more memorable victories of patriotic weakness over aggressive strength. The humble pikemen defended themselves with desperation against the charges of the French knights, and at last threw them into disorder against a marshy stream, where they butchered them without quarter. The battle is called that of the Golden Spurs, because of the enormous number of gold spurs collected after it from the feet of slain French nobles. It has ever since been one of the greatest patriotic memories of Flemish Belgium; and as such was recalled by King Albert in August 1914, in his proclamation to his people on the German invasion.

Flanders was thus saved at the critical moment from annexation by the French monarchy, and was saved by the artisans, not the nobles. So opened the fourteenth century. In about the same time that it took the England of William the Conqueror to become the England of Edward I, the Flemish towns which at the battle of Cassel had first shown feudalism that they were a force, had gained strength to defeat the most powerful of European monarchies. The leading town at the earlier period was Ypres; and down to the thirteenth century this was the centre of the Flemish cloth trade. Its great hall of the Clothworkers' Guild, built early in that century in the finest period of Gothic, remains still (or remained till the German bombardment of 1914) the noblest piece of architecture designed for a civic purpose in Belgium, and perhaps in Europe. And it symbolises a very notable thing, which the Flemish cloth trade initiated in the modern world; namely, international commerce not in aristocratic luxuries (such as the silks and jewels and spices which Venice and Genoa shipped from the Levant, or the suits of fine armour and swords which some towns manufactured for foreign kings and nobles), but in a relatively cheap manufactured article of common, and ultimately universal, use. Manufacture and wholesale trade as a means of raising the material comfort and welfare of masses of men first appears north of the Alps in the Flemish cities; and in them the great guild system (adopted from them in mediæval England, France, Brabant, and Germany) had its first and most powerful development.

A contingent from Ypres was prominent at the Battle of the Spurs; indeed, its special heroism decided the result. But for some time before this the primacy of Ypres had passed to the great rivals, Bruges and Ghent; and it is they who dominate the fourteenth century, the most glorious of Flemish epochs. The commanding figure of this age is Jacobus Van Artevelde of Ghent, who directed the policy of that city from 1336 to 1345. His story, like that of his son, comes before the literary world in the pages of the most celebrated of mediæval chroniclers, Froissart, who was a native of Valenciennes, till three centuries later a Belgian town; but much new light has been thrown on it by the researches of modern Belgian historians into the civic archives of the period. The struggle between the French monarchy and the Flemish burghers was renewed actively after the accession in 1322 of Louis de Nevers (a prince brought up at the French court) as Count of Flanders. He had not reigned long before the citizens of Bruges and Courtrai rose against him and took him prisoner. Influenced by French threats, and also by a quarrel with Ghent, they set him free, and he resumed his position; but soon afterwards there was a second rising, which drove him out of the country. The French king, Philip of Valois, intervened with a large army, and at Cassel inflicted a crushing defeat on the burgher levies, who were commanded by a popular leader, Nicholas Zannekin. This was in the very year of Philip's accession to the French throne—an accession disputed by Edward III of England, who claimed that he had a better right through his mother. While, therefore, the battle of Cassel reduced the Flemish to subjection under Louis de Nevers and France, they would now have a potential ally against France, if they rebelled, in the person of Edward III. Perhaps it was because an English alliance had twice in the previous century proved a broken reed that they did not at first respond to Edward III's advances. In 1336 Edward resolved to force them to show their hand, and accordingly prohibited the export of wool from England. Deprived of its main supply of raw material, the Flemish weaving industry underwent a severe crisis of depression and unemployment; and during this Jacobus Van Artevelde came to the front. Legend, which has described him to us as low-born and a brewer, is certainly wrong on the first point and probably on the second. His father was a great cloth merchant and held the high office of *Échevin* at Ghent, an office which was hereditary in a few patrician families. Jacobus himself married a famous knight's daughter, and was always treated by Edward III and the other great personages of the day with the utmost personal respect. Yet he differed from them, because he was not a feudal lord, but a civic statesman. It was as an orator and political leader that for nine years he ruled his native Ghent, and for a shorter period brought all the chief communes of Flanders into a league that, had it lasted, might have made Flanders a nation. He took the lead at Ghent about 1336. In 1337 an English fleet destroyed the navy of mercenary warships (chiefly Genoese), with which Louis de Nevers blockaded Bruges and Ghent and controlled their commerce. In 1338 Ghent, Bruges, and Ypres rose against their Count; a punitive expedition by the French king failed; and Louis de Nevers had to give in, and swear to observe the constitutions and charters of Flanders. In June of that year treaties were signed between the Flemish city communes and both England and France, whereby the Flemings secured the right to trade freely in both countries, and were not bound to fight with either on behalf of the other. This was a great achievement of Van Artevelde's statesmanship, and at once restored to Flanders its commercial prosperity. But it was not what either of the rival military monarchies wanted; and in the following year the flight of Louis de Nevers to Paris, followed by a French invasion and devastation of Flanders, compelled the Ghent statesman to become Edward III's ally. A treaty was negotiated at Brussels between Edward III of England, John III, Duke of Brabant, and the

seven principal communes of Flanders—
Ghent, Bruges, Ypres, Courtrai, Alost, Oudenarde, and Grammont. Edward III proceeded
to Ghent, and by Van Artevelde's advice was
proclaimed King of France, and received the
homage of the Flemings in that capacity.
Next spring (1340) the Hundred Years War
between England and France began.

The first great event of the war, the decisive English naval victory over the French
at Sluys (1340), was materially due to the
men of Bruges, who (somewhat like the
Prussians at Waterloo) intervened decisively
at the critical end of a long struggle. After
this the sea passage between England and
Flanders was secure; and Edward III, with
Flanders as a base and Flemish wealth to
pay his way, waged annual campaigns against
the French. Unfortunately for Van Artevelde, who was the life and soul of the Anglo-
Flemish alliance, no striking success was
obtained in them; and as time went by,
the weak points of the Flemish burghers,
their short-sighted parsimony and factious
partisanship, reasserted themselves against
his influence. Van Artevelde stood for a
great idea, the independence of the Flemish
communes secured by harmony and a de-
fensive alliance between them. But his

fellow Flemings saw more clearly that he
stood for paying subsidies to Edward III
and for interfering with the sacred right of
one Flemish city to wage selfish and interne-
cine strife with another. Already in 1343
he was formally accused of seeking to be a
military dictator, but the Ghent Council
acquitted him. Nevertheless he could not
prevent repeated wars from breaking out
between the communes, nor even the feuds
between the different guilds in Ghent itself
from developing into pitched battles on the
city market-place. Such fights between
guilds were the guild equivalent of modern
trade disputes; and they raged fiercely at
this time between the weavers' guild, who
represented the aristocracy of Ghent industry, and the fullers' guild, who represented a humbler class of labourers. If we
remember that Van Artevelde's father was
a great weaver and he himself a leading
patrician, we may perhaps find here an important explanation of his fall. At any
rate in July 1345, when the animosity between the weavers and fullers was hottest,
a riot broke out against him in the streets,
his house was attacked by the mob, and he
was murdered. So fell one of the greatest
of mediæval statesmen, a man much in

advance of his time, who aimed not only at achieving the independence of Flanders, but at establishing security for the new industrial civilisation of the cities against the forces of feudal and monarchical militarism which raged outside their walls. In 1346, the year after his death, Edward III won the battle of Crécy. Had he won it but fifteen months earlier, Van Artevelde might very well have lived to alter the whole history not only of Flanders, but of Western culture.

Van Artevelde's projects, though novel, were not Utopian. The Flemings had resources enough to attain them, could they only have made a disciplined and concerted use of what they had. It must be remembered that Ghent alone possessed in the first Van Artevelde's time perhaps a quarter of a million population, or three times that of London; and the realisable wealth in Flanders not only vastly surpassed that of England, but probably exceeded that of France. Add that the Flemings were good fighters, and supplied mercenaries to many European wars. But after Van Artevelde's death the political greatness of their cities steadily declined. They suffered severely from the Black Death, that memorable plague which

shook all European society; and then were
engaged for some decades in struggles with
their Count, Louis de Mâle, who was the
son of Louis de Nevers and continued to
pursue, with more astuteness, all the worst
aims of his tyrant father's policy. Edward
III took advantage of the troubles to invite
large numbers of Flemish craftsmen to settle
in England, which they enriched by establishing the cloth manufacture; but the selfish-
ness of the communes after Jacobus Van
Artevelde's death steadily alienated the
King from effective alliance. In 1369 Louis
de Mâle's daughter and heiress was married
to the Duke of Burgundy (the brother of
the then King of France), and the courts of
France, Burgundy, and Flanders adopted a
common policy, directed against the liberty
of the communes. Bruges in the hands of
the " Leliaerts " became the military base
of the Count; the artisans of Ghent fought
the last battles for freedom. There was a
moment in 1379 when Ghent had rallied
nearly all the cities to her side, and Louis
de Mâle, closely besieged in Oudenarde,
came to terms with his opponents. But
as soon as he was free he tore up the agree-
ment, fled to France, returned with an army,
and within a few months, by a mixture of

intrigue and force had recovered every town
in Flanders but Ghent. He then twice (1380
and 1381) attacked Ghent itself; and though
baffled by the fortifications, inflicted a crushing defeat on the city's field army at Nevele.
Ghent was practically blockaded, and famine
was in prospect. There was no chance of
foreign help, for the conflict had assumed a
clearly revolutionary character, as a struggle
between feudalism and the communes; and
not only were similar struggles simultaneously
in progress in Brabant (between the Duke
and the commune of Louvain) and in France
(between the King and the commune of
Paris), but England itself under Richard II
was in the throes of revolutionary movements.
In its agony Ghent turned to Philip Van
Artevelde, the son of the great Jacobus;
and with bitter contrition for his father's
murder appointed him " First Captain of
the City of Ghent " and " Regent of Flanders "
(January 1382). There is nothing to show
that Philip was a man of genius, but he did
his best in a desperate situation. He first
tried to obtain terms for the starving city
from the Count, but failed; and then made
a sortie with a picked force of something
over 5000 men against the Count's army
at Bruges. Though outnumbered by over

seven to one, the Ghent burghers won a complete victory, followed immediately by their capture of Bruges and the revictualling of their own population. But unfortunately Louis de Mâle himself, though chased and hard pressed, escaped in disguise and made his way again to France. In November of the same year a great French feudal army, commanded by the King but directed by the military talents of Oliver de Clisson, Constable of France, marched into Flanders to crush the rebel artisans. The Flemings were outgeneralled by De Clisson; they lost two battles; and at the second and greatest, the battle of Roosebeke (November 27, 1382), Philip Van Artevelde and 25,000 Flemings were slain. The French King did not besiege Ghent, but after sacking Courtrai returned to Paris to crush the commune there; and with English assistance the Ghent burghers held out against Louis de Mâle till his death fourteen months later. But the hope of freedom for the Flemish city-commonwealths was gone. What the battle of the Golden Spurs began, the catastrophe of Roosebeke fatally ended; Ghent had made the great refusal thirty-seven years earlier, when Jacobus Van Artevelde was murdered; and not all its belated heroism under his son could avert the consequences.

The epoch of the Arteveldes, whose story we have briefly summarised, left a mark on the Low Countries which has never been wholly effaced. To this day it is impossible without some knowledge of it to penetrate the soul of modern Belgium. In three ways particularly is its effect felt. In the first place it has given local feeling and municipal patriotism a peculiar intensity. An inhabitant of Ghent or Bruges, Courtrai or Ypres, Brussels or Antwerp, is apt still to think of his city first and his country afterwards; and the Burgomasters and *Échevins* of the modern towns, though very different functionaries from their mediæval namesakes, have an extraordinary hold on the imagination of the people—alike in constitutional crises and in the German invasion of 1914 they have often seemed the firmest rallying-points in Belgian society. Secondly, it is above all in the history and tradition of this period that the Belgians have their national epic, their treasure of national romance. The tangle of wars and rivalries, in which at times the hand of almost every Flemish town seems against that of every other, are an inexhaustible mine of human

interest; and they are so because with all
their blindness and final failure the forces
at work were new forces; there was a genuine
upheaval of human life from the depths,
with that note of freshness and exhilaration
which goes with the perceiving of new
horizons. Thirdly, the memory of the men
of that time has always been an assurance
to their descendants—even in the darkest
hours of their subsequent oppression and
humiliation during the centuries when
Belgium was the "cockpit of Europe"—
that they are a great people and a distinct
people. But for it their nationality could
never have risen triumphant from its grave,
as during the nineteenth century it did.

The history of Brabant in the thirteenth
and fourteenth centuries ran a course parallel
to that of Flanders. The struggle between
feudalism and the communes was similar,
though on a smaller scale and freer from
foreign interference. The victory of Duke
John I at Woeringen (1288) over a German
coalition confirmed Brabant's independence
against German aggression; just as the
victory of the Golden Spurs, fourteen years
later, confirmed that of Flanders against
French. But Woeringen was won by the
nobles on behalf of the people, not by the

people fighting against the nobles. One
other date must be noted as a landmark
for future constitutional development, the
Joyous Entry of Duke Wenceslas (1356).
"Joyous Entries" into their principal
towns, Louvain and Brussels, were a regular
part of the accession ceremonies of the
Dukes of Brabant; and were usually signalised
by their confirming or granting whatever
charters or privileges the citizens had or
could extort. Wenceslas was a foreigner,
who married the heiress of the last native
duke; and perhaps for this reason the
charter of his Joyous Entry, though it contained no new liberties, was a specially
thorough ratification of those previously
conceded. As time went on, it became
for Brabant what Magna Charta and the
Habeas Corpus Act were for England; and
owing to the later prominence of Brabant
as the metropolitan province, it was this,
and not the charters of Flanders, which
formed the main basis of modern Belgian
constitutional liberty.

If the fourteenth century is dominated
by the great communes, the fifteenth is
dominated by the House of Burgundy,
under whom the germs of a national idea
were first developed. Though these princes,

like the Habsburgs later, were foreigners,
they acquired their position by marriage
through the failure of native dynasties in
the male line; and they came to develop a
decidedly national policy for their Belgian
subjects. They ruthlessly crushed, it is true,
the liberties of the communes; but partly,
at least, because those liberties in their
particularist form seemed to make it impossible either to preserve the internal peace
of the country or to organise its defence
against foreign aggression. Philip the Good
(1419–1467) first united all the provinces,
including Holland, under a single rule; and
in his long reign went a long way towards
founding a new monarchy, which should
be independent of France or Germany,
and whose centre of gravity should be in
Flanders and Brabant. If his hand was
heavy on the political privileges of the
cities, their commercial, industrial, and
artistic activities flourished under his sway.
Bruges, as a semi-royal capital and the seat
of the Order of the Golden Fleece, enjoyed
its last great prosperity; Ghent, in spite
of its terrible chastisement in 1453 at the
battle of Gavre, maintained its population
and wealth; Brabant for the first time
began to catch Flanders up, and the wonder-

ful town halls of Brussels and Louvain are
the surviving record of their new civic
magnificence. From this period dates the
University of Louvain (founded 1425); from
this period too, the commencement of
Antwerp Cathedral, and the rise of Antwerp
itself as a great port. Philip was an enlightened patron of the arts; he not only
encouraged fine buildings, but he took the
brothers Van Eyck, the greatest of Primitive
Flemish painters, under his personal patron-
age; and it was under his sway that the
painting of the Low Countries first gave
promise of the place which it was destined
to fill in the artistic achievement of the
world. In short his reign, which coincides
with the introduction of printing and the
first advent of the Greek Renaissance, ex-
hibits more wealth, more splendour and
refinement, more intellectual and artistic
work within the Belgian provinces than
ever before. After the death of his son
Charles the Bold in circumstances which
ended for ever the dream of a Burgundian
kingdom, the communes underwent for
some years vicissitudes of freedom and sup-
pression. They first (1477) extorted from
his orphan daughter, Mary, the " Great
Privilege," a restoration of all their charters

and liberties. It was accompanied by the
convening of a States-General, a sort of
Parliament; whose development, though of
more capital importance for the history of
Holland, had its consequences also for that
of Belgium. Later on, Mary's widower,
the Archduke Maximilian of Austria, afterwards Emperor, took away most of these
concessions by the Treaties of Damme (1490)
and Cadzand (1492), after protracted conflicts with both Ghent and Bruges. But,
though the greatness of Bruges passed to
Antwerp, the wealth of the Low Countries
continued to increase. Finally the accession
in 1506 of the Emperor Charles V (born at
Ghent in 1500) gave them a prince, whom
their people could regard as a native, and
who amid multifarious campaigns and the
cares of a motley empire greater than any
since the decline of Rome always took an
especial pride in the provinces, which were
his earliest dominion and to the last brought
him his greatest wealth. Under the Re-
gencies of his aunt, Margaret of Austria,
and his sister, Mary Queen of Hungary,
Belgium reached the climax of its prosperity.
The Low Countries were then organised as
a single dominion of seventeen provinces,
there being added to the nine of Belgium

the seven which make modern Holland,
and Artois, which is now part of France.
The nine were not quite the same as to-day,
East and West Flanders forming one province,
while Malines (Mechlin) was the centre of a
province to-day merged in those of Brabant
and Antwerp. Brussels, owing to its central
position, became the capital and seat of
government for the whole. Another important step was the institution of a national
Privy Council. This was formed in 1517,
when Charles V, already ruler of the Low
Countries in person, went away to Spain
to receive the crown of Aragon and take
over the government in succession to his
grandfather Ferdinand. At first a temporary
body, it was constituted of Knights of the
Golden Fleece (the famous Order established
at Bruges by Philip the Good), combined
with leading members of a Council of the
States which met at Malines. Several times
reappointed after brief intervals, the Council
became permanent; and together with the
central administration which (under the
Regent) it controlled, exerted a powerful
unifying effect over the entire Netherlands.
In 1531 it was constituted in three collateral
bodies—a Council of State, a Privy Council,
and a Council of Finance; and this triple

constitution lasted, with a few brief inter-ruptions, for two centuries and a half.

Charles V's Government was harassed by repeated unsuccessful attempts on the part of the French monarchy to annex Artois and Flanders. There was also a famous revolt of Ghent in 1539, crushed by Charles in 1540. But in spite of these troubles the country reached the high-water mark of its prosperity. The Belgians carried on in the sixteenth century a far greater trade than any people had before, for there was concentrated in their hands what in the seventeenth century was divided between the Dutch, the English and the French. It is said that nearly 500 of the light vessels of those times entered and left the port of Antwerp daily, and it did more business in a month than Venice did in two years. The old staple products of the Flemish looms, their unrivalled cloths and linens, came to be exported far beyond the confines of Europe; but besides them a host of special industries had grown up in textiles and metals. It was now that the carpets of Brussels, the tapestries of Arras, the cannon of Mons and Liége, the gloves of Louvain, the lace of Malines, and a great many localised types of velvet, silk, embroidery, and damask

enjoyed their highest reputation. The lead
of the Belgian cities over the other European
capitals is well expressed by the punning
remark of Charles V to the French King,
Francis I : " I could put your Paris inside
my Ghent " (the French for " Ghent " and
" glove " are the same in pronunciation).
Yet Ghent, though large, had declined from
its fourteenth-century size; the leading
city now was Antwerp, with perhaps a
quarter of a million inhabitants. Ghent
came next with about two-thirds of the
population of Antwerp, and Liége (still
separate under its Prince-Bishop) next again.
Brussels, though a fine city and the capital
of the provinces, had perhaps not over a
third of the population of Antwerp. London
in the Emperor Charles V's time was about
on the scale of Brussels; it grew much under
Queen Elizabeth, and in 1590 the Italian
writer, Giovanni Botero, classed it as the
equal of Ghent with about 160,000 inhabitants.
No other English town was in the sixteenth
century comparable to the great cities of
Belgium.

CHAPTER V

THE HISTORIC SUBJECTION OF BELGIUM

No one could appreciate the sentiment of
the Belgian nation regarding its unity and
independence without some understanding of
its sufferings during the three hundred and
seventy-five years of its subjection to foreign
rule. The first act in this long tragedy, the
reign of Philip II of Spain, is fairly well known
to English and American readers through the
works of Motley. The later developments
during the long period when Belgium was
fought over and torn in pieces by the Powers,
like a bone by quarrelling dogs, have been less
vividly realised. True, some of the masters
of English literature, such as Sterne and
Thackeray, have thrown a picturesque light
round British campaigns in the country;
but, like the campaigners, they gave little
notice to the inhabitants, and what they
did give is sometimes very unfair.

The period 1555–1830 falls into six sections :

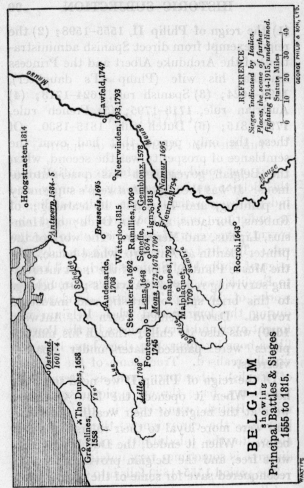

BELGIUM
showing
Principal Battles & Sieges
1555 to 1815.

REFERENCE
Sieges indicated by *Italics*.
Places, the scene of further
fighting 1914-1915, underlined.
Statute Miles
0   10   20   30   40

GEORGE PHILIP & SON, LTD.

Hoogstraeten,1814

o Lawfeld,1747

Neerwinden,1693,1793

o *Antwerp*,1584-5

Brussels,1695

Gemblours,1578

Waterloo,1815

Ramillies,1706

Namur, 1695

Audenarde,
1708

Senefe,
1674

Ligny,1815

Fleurus, 1794

Steenkerke,1692

Lens,1648

Mons,1572,1678,1709

Jemappes,1792

Malplaquet,
1709

Ostend,
1601-4

Fontenoy,
1745

Lille,1708

x The Dunes, 1658

Gravelines,
1558

Rocroi,1643 o

Meuse

Meuse

Meuse

Schelde

Yse

Lys

Sambre

Yser

WAXTYPE

(1) the reign of Philip II, 1555–1598; (2) the reign (exempt from direct Spanish administration) of the Archduke Albert and the Princess Isabella, his wife (Philip II's daughter), 1599–1624; (3) Spanish rule, 1624–1713; (4) Austrian rule, 1713–1795; (5) French rule, 1795–1815; (6) Dutch rule, 1815–1830. Of these the only period that had even the semblance of prosperity was the second, when the Belgian government was quasi-autonomous. It was the age of Antwerp's supremacy in painting, and Louvain's in learning; of Rubens, Jordaens, and Van Dyck; of Heinsius, Lipsius, and Mercator. The work of the printer Plantin at Antwerp, whose house, now the Musée Plantin, is one of the most interesting surviving relics of that city's past, belongs to this brief spell of artistic and industrial revival. David Teniers (born at Antwerp 1610) was also its child; though his masterpieces were painted later under Spanish viceroys.

Of the reign of Philip II we need say little here. When it opened, the Low Countries were at the height of their wealth and fame, and were more loyal to their rulers than ever before. When it ended, the Dutch provinces were free, and the Belgian provinces, though reconquered save for some of the coast towns,

had been devastated by thirty years of war
and nearly forty of religious persecution.
Already, before Alva's arrival (1567), some
30,000 Belgian refugees had fled to England;
during his seven years' rule those who perished
at the scaffold or stake are said to have exceeded 18,000; to the latter figure must be
added not only the victims of his battles, but
those of the merciless sacking of Mons, Malines,
and other places. After Alva's departure,
the terrible mutiny of the Spanish troops
(who massacred 6000 people at Antwerp in
the " Spanish Fury " of 1576), and the long
wars of Don John of Austria and the Prince
of Parma with their many famous battles
and sieges, had been added to the bloody
record. There are no total figures, but it
seems likely that the population was reduced
by at least 50 per cent. The permanent
wealth of the country declined even more.
Throughout the period there was an unceasing
outflow of many of the most active industrial
elements to England and Holland. The
trading prosperity of Amsterdam and Rotterdam not merely followed on the decline of
Antwerp and Ghent, but was in considerable
part the work of refugees from those places.
Protestantism in Belgium was completely
stamped out; only Roman Catholics were

left living. As the Dutch were almost as ruthless in persecuting the Roman Catholics, a hard-and-fast division was created between the Dutch and Belgians, which brought to nothing repeated attempts (especially in 1576, and again as late as 1632) to unite the two peoples in one independent State.

The joint reign of Albert and Isabella was, as we have said, a brighter interlude. They ruled not as the tools of Madrid, but as quasi-independent sovereigns. Unfortunately, more than a third of their joint reign was blighted by the war with the Dutch, which was waged principally on Belgian soil, and included some of the most desperate feats in the military history of the Low Countries, such as the three years' siege of Ostend. In 1621 the Archduke Albert died childless; and in accordance with Philip II's original deed of cession to his daughter and son-in-law Belgium reverted to the Spanish Crown. The formal transfer was effected in 1624; and the speedy return of Spanish abuses, followed by French and Dutch wars, submerged the brief sunset splendour of the age of Rubens. Nevertheless, the work of the men of that age, and not least the Titanic effort of Rubens himself, has remained and still remains one of the chief sources of pride and inspiration to the Belgian people. Its gospel is essentially of the Renaissance and Pagan, a gospel of human (and especially physical) development and enjoyment; but it was translated with such amazing power by the paintings of Rubens and Jordaens into the very idiom of Flemish taste and feeling that the translation became virtually a new work, a revelation to the Belgian people of forces within themselves, which had never before found such mighty expression. What the genius of Shakespeare has been to the English nation, that, it is scarcely too much to say, the creative energy of Rubens has been to the Flemings.

Already since Alva's time Belgium had been becoming the " cockpit of Europe." French, English, and Dutch all used it as their battle-ground against Spain, with German and Austrian troops coming in as Spain's auxiliaries. But in the 130 years which followed the Archduke Albert's death, this hardship reached its climax. Most of the wars waged in West Europe were waged by or against the ambitious French monarchy, with Holland first as its ally, later as the centre of resistance to it. As Belgium lay between France and Holland, and belonged throughout to one or other of France's Continental rivals, Spain and Austria, her soil was the inevitable meeting-ground of their armies; besides being particularly accessible to oversea intervention from England. Its extensive plains were well suited for pitched battles of the old one-day type; but its lack of natural obstacles caused it to be heavily fortified, and it became above all celebrated for siege warfare.

How this struck a contemporary may be curiously seen from an old English book, *Instructions for Forreine Travell*, written by James Howell, a clerk in the diplomatic service, in 1642. After taking his traveller to Italy, and bringing him back across the Alps through " the Cantons, those rugged Republics," and " the stately proud cities of Germany," Howell conducts him to Brussels,

and there he shall behold the face of a constant Military Court and Provincial Government, with a miscellany of all nations; *and if there be any leaguers* (*i.e.* sieges) *afoot or armies in motion, it should be time well spent to see them.* For the Netherlands have been for many years, as one may say, the very cockpit of Christendom, the school of arms and rendezvous of all adventurous spirits and cadets; which makes most nations beholden to them for soldiers. Therefore the history of the Belgic wars are very worth the reading; for I know none fuller of stratagems, of reaches of policy, of variety of successes in so short a time : nor in which more princes have been engaged for reasons of State, *nor a war which hath produced such deplorable effects, directly or collaterally, all Christendom over, both by sea and land.*

The very *naïveté* of this passage is informing. Howell has been pointing out the things of note in each country; and when he comes to Belgium, he takes as the only thing worth mentioning its permanent " military court " and standing army of mercenaries drawn from all nations; adding, as the characteristic spectacle, with which the country may be expected to regale the sightseer, sieges and campaigns ! Already it is known as the " cockpit of Christendom "; already its war is a by-word as having produced the " most deplorable effects " ever recorded. And yet in 1642 the great battles and sieges on Belgian soil, by which Condé and Turenne, William III and Marshal Luxembourg, the great fortress-engineer Vauban, Marlborough and Prince Eugène, and Marshal Saxe made the greater part of their military reputations, lay still in the future. So did the later campaigns of Jemmappes, Neerwinden, Fleurus, and Waterloo.

The miseries which this situation entailed

on the natives of the country may be better
imagined than described. The armies of the
seventeenth and eighteenth centuries were
composed of mercenaries. Not only was it
the regular policy of commanders to " live
on the country," but a certain amount of
loot and rape was regarded by the individual
soldier as one of the recognised rewards of his
adventurous calling. Armies mutinied if
they were not from time to time given a town
or a village to sack. But in these Belgian
wars the country on which *both* sides lived
was the Belgian country, the towns which
both armies sacked were the Belgian towns.
Small wonder if the people were not only
impoverished but brutalised, if their traditional
hospitality gave way to a sullen and almost
impartial dislike of all foreigners, if they were
driven back on themselves into a gloomy and
crafty egotism, clinging desperately to the
municipal privileges and local liberties, which
alone were left them out of the wreck. A
weaker people would have been exterminated.
The Belgians by sheer pertinacity survived,
their patient industry working without rest
to repair the wounds which devastation and
rapine inflicted.

Just as Belgium in the seventeenth century
was the theatre of most European wars, so its
towns and provinces were the small change

D 2

of most diplomatic negotiations. The national heritage was considerably pared down in the process. By the Treaty of the Pyrenees (1659) Louis XIV annexed to France nearly the whole province of Artois, with the important town of Arras. At the Peace of Aix-la-Chapelle (1668) he got his hand into Flanders and Hainaut, taking the towns and districts of Douai, Lille, Courtrai, Oudenarde, and Charleroi. By the Peace of Nimeguen (1679) he gave back Courtrai, Oudenarde, and Charleroi, but took Valenciennes, Cambrai, St. Omer, Ypres, and Nieuport instead. By the Peace of Ryswick (1697) he gave up Ypres and Nieuport, and the frontier was determined much as it is now. As the net result of his various aggressions he had added to the permanent territory of France not only Artois, with the town of Arras, but the important strip of Flanders and Hainaut, including Dunkirk, St. Omer, Lille, Roubaix, Valenciennes, and Cambrai. His gains now form the French department of the Nord, with most of that of the Pas-de-Calais, and they comprise one of the most important coal-mining and manufacturing districts of France. Thus was last settled the nationality of a region which had been debated in war for centuries. The military prominence which this very region has reassumed in the fighting of 1914–1915 is a striking example of the way in which the strategical consequences entailed by a geographical position re-assert themselves over long periods of time.

The most famous Belgian battles of Louis XIV's period are perhaps worth briefly enumerating. They were : *Honnecourt* (1642), where the long-invincible " Spanish infantry " (chiefly composed of Walloons) won its last great victory over the French : *Rocroi* (1643), where the celebrated Prince of Condé (then Duc d'Enghien) gained the first of a series of French victories, by which the credit of the Spanish infantry was destroyed ; *Lens* (1648), a repetition by Condé of his victory at Rocroi ; *the Dunes* (1658), in which the Spanish were defeated by Turenne, the second of Louis XIV's world-famous generals, with the powerful assistance of 5000 of Cromwell's English veterans ; *Seneffe* (1674), where the youthful Prince of Orange, afterwards William III of England, was defeated by the veteran Condé ; *Steenkerke* (1692), in which a large mixed army of Dutch, Germans, Spanish, and English under William III was defeated by the French Marshal Luxembourg ; *Neerwinden* or Landen (1693), in which William III was again defeated by the same opponent ; *Ramillies* (1706), in which the English and Dutch allies

under the Duke of Marlborough defeated the
French under Marshal Villeroi; *Oudenarde*
(1708), in which Marlborough and Prince
Eugène of Savoy defeated the French under
the Dukes of Burgundy and Vendôme; and
Malplaquet (1709), in which Marlborough and
Eugène obtained a Pyrrhic victory over the
French Marshal Villars. But this list of battles
gives only a faint idea of the number and extent
of the campaigns. Those were above all the
days of endless marches and counter-marches,
entrenchments and counter-entrenchments,
and of Fabian tactics, whose object was to
cause the distress and dissolution of the
enemy's mercenary army without incurring
the hazard and losses of a general action.
There were generals then like William III;
who earned a formidable military reputation
by these methods, although in every one of his
great pitched battles on the Continent he was
defeated. There were literally scores of important sieges; those best-known to English
readers are William III's siege of Namur (for
which see Sterne's *Tristram Shandy*), and
Marlborough's sieges of Lille, Tournai, and
Mons; but perhaps the most cruel to Belgian
sentiment was Marshal Villeroi's devastating
bombardment of Brussels (1695). Many of
these names serve to emphasise afresh the
identity of Louis XIV's battle-grounds with

those of the 1914–1915 war. The showing of history is that any conflicts, in which the hegemony of Europe is sought, whether by Spain, France, or Germany, are almost bound to be fought on this area. If the Napoleonic Wars before 1815 seem an exception, it is only an apparent one; the truth being that the French Republic by its annexation of Belgium in 1795 had already tipped the balance of Europe heavily in France's favour. The only reason why Napoleon had not to fight for this advantage was that his immediate predecessors had secured it in advance. The campaign of 1815, on the other hand, showed the normal development of the game when the pieces started fair on the chessboard.

By the Treaty of Utrecht (1713), what were left of the unhappy Belgian provinces were transferred from Spain to Austria. They were well rid of the Spaniards, who when strong had mercilessly oppressed them, and when weak had left them helplessly exposed to French and Dutch invasions. The Austrians proved a little better in both respects. Their first agent in Belgium, the Piedmontese Marquis de Prié (he was deputy for the nominal governor, Prince Eugène), believed in using the iron hand; but after his time for nearly sixty years a lighter rule was the practice. With their town trade destroyed and strangled, the people fell back on agriculture. It is now that the closeness of peasant cultivation in Flanders begins. Unfortunately the first great European War after the Peace of Utrecht—the war between England and Austria on the one side, and France and Prussia on the other over the question of the Austrian succession and Frederick the Great's seizure of Silesia—made Belgium a "cockpit" again. In 1744 the French invaded the provinces; in 1745, under Marshal Saxe, they won the famous victory of Fontenoy over the Anglo-German army commanded by the Duke of Cumberland; in 1747 Marshal Saxe besieged and captured Brussels, and won another great victory at Lawfeld. Fontenoy and Lawfeld are of historic interest to the Anglo-Celtic peoples, because on each occasion the English infantry fought with extraordinary courage and credit against superior forces of French, and on each the victory was won for the latter very largely by the heroism of their Irish Brigade. But to the Belgians it was only the renewal of their old misery. The French occupied the country as invaders for two years, and thoroughly plundered it by all kinds of official extortions. In 1748, by the Peace of Aix-la-Chapelle, it was given back to Austria.

The experience of this war disinclined

Austria to spend money or take trouble over a country so easily lost to her. Thenceforward the Habsburgs chiefly valued Belgium as a possible asset for dynastic bargaining. They made indeed persistent, though unsuccessful efforts to exchange it for Silesia or Bavaria. However, in the Seven Years War (1756–1763) save for one small raid, it escaped fighting. This singular immunity was due to the fact that, for the first time for centuries, Austria and France were in alliance. Moreover the Empress Maria Theresa appointed as governor for the greater part of her reign a decidedly sympathetic ruler, her brother-in-law, Prince Charles of Lorraine. She also repudiated and got rid of the pretensions of England and Holland to strangle, under the Treaties of Ryswick and Utrecht, the trade of Belgium with France. Her son Joseph II went further; he took advantage of the war made by Holland on England (at the time of the American War of Independence) to turn out the Dutch garrisons, which by those treaties were entitled to occupy the Belgian fortresses on the French frontier. Their expulsion was really an important step in the clearing of Belgium from foreign claims; though as Joseph II in order to secure the assent of France was obliged not to garrison the fortresses with Austrians or Belgians but to dismantle them altogether, the immediate effect was to facilitate the invasion of Belgium by the armies of the French Republic ten years later.

Before this invasion an event occurred, which had an important influence on the eventual re-birth of Belgium as a nation. This was the Brabant Revolution of 1789–1790 when the people of Brabant, Flanders, and Hainaut rose against Austria, expelled the Austrian garrisons, and set up a " United States of Belgium," which lasted for a good part of a year. Undoubtedly the success then obtained against the Austrians encouraged the successful rising against the Dutch forty years later. But the Revolution was not a handsome affair in itself. The first cause of discontent was Joseph II's admirable and enlightened Edict of Tolerance, which permitted the private exercise of their religion to all Lutherans, Calvinists, and Greek Christians within the Austrian dominions, and made them eligible for public offices. The Emperor went on to decree reforms abolishing superfluous convents, and establishing " grand seminaries " at Louvain and Luxemburg, through which all candidates for the clergy were to pass. At the same time he attempted changes in civil administration ; but it was not these which aroused the

revolt. Three centuries of severe penalties
on unorthodoxy had made the Belgians an
intensely clerical people. The Pope had
sanctioned the Edict of Tolerance, but they
were more Catholic than the Pope. Their
formal appeal was, as usual, to their old
charters, and particularly to the " Joyous
Entry " of Wenceslas (Duke of Brabant
1356–1383), which was the great charter of
Brussels, Louvain, and the other Brabant towns.
These charters were granted at a time when
Roman Catholicism was the only known form
of Christian religion ; and it was comparatively
easy to use their phrases in a sense adverse
to any other.

Begun in clericalism, the Revolution speedily
grew into oligarchy and tyranny. Its outbreak was successful through the joint efforts
of two bodies—a party of nobles with the
Duc d'Arenberg and other chiefs of the
Belgian aristocracy at their head, and a more
popular party headed by an advocate, Henri
Van der Noot. After their victory the
two parties started quarrelling, and Van der
Noot, a " tyrant " in the Greek sense, became
a sort of dictator. The whole movement
was much influenced by the revolutionary
events in Paris, from the fall of the Bastille
onwards ; but the extremely conservative
Belgians were not really in tune with Parisian

aspirations. Van der Noot soon made himself disliked; in November 1790 the Emperor Leopold, who had succeeded Joseph II on the throne of Austria, sent an army forward; and it reconquered the country very quickly with but little resistance. It is worth noting that in 1789 a revolution broke out also in Liége, still outside the Belgian territory. The people rose against their Prince-Bishop, and claimed the same rights as the French revolutionists. Their brief success was ended by Leopold's army, which restored the Prince-Bishop.

But the dominance of Austria in Belgium was now drawing to its close. In 1792 war broke out between the Habsburgs and the young French Republic. Belgium was twice invaded, and in the autumn the French under Dumouriez won the battle of Jemmappes (November 6). As the barrier fortresses had been dismantled, this victory gave the French the country. They were first welcomed as liberators; but their excesses (they set up the guillotine at Brussels and started wholesale confiscations) soon alienated the Belgians. The next year the Austrians reappeared, defeated the French at Neerwinden, and won everything back. In 1794 the French invaded Belgium again, and the Austrians decided in the interests of their strategy as a whole to evacuate it. They were defeated at Fleurus, and the French reconquered both Belgium and Liége. Fortunately for the Belgians the task was not completed till Robespierre had fallen and the Reign of Terror was over. They had been thrice conquered in three years; and their status was uncertain for nearly a year more, during which they suffered a good deal of confiscation and squeezing; but in 1795 they were formally incorporated, with Liége, in the French Republic. Their time-honoured constitutions and charters, which (though too often broken) were in principle the most liberal on the Continent before 1789, were ruthlessly swept away.

From that time until 1814 the French were masters of Belgium, which shared the vicissitudes of the Directory, the Consulate, and the Empire. The new rulers conferred one great benefit; they saved the country from becoming the " cockpit " of the greatest wars, which till then the world had known. They introduced the Code Napoléon, which the country still uses; and at intervals their administration, and still more the personality of Napoleon, were decidedly popular. Moreover, they opened the Schelde; though, except during the two brief years when France was at peace with England, this was practically nullified by the blockade of the English Fleet. But the conscription which they introduced was intensely disliked—in 1798 there was a desperate revolt of the rural poor against it, the so-called "Peasants War"; and as the Napoleonic struggles imposed heavier and heavier exactions both in men and money, the Emperor's early popularity (at its height when he visited the country in 1803) disappeared. Yet in 1813, after his defeat at Leipzig, there was no revolt against him in Belgium as there was in Holland. It remained for the Prussian General Bülow, after his victory at Hoogstraeten (January 1814), to expel Napoleon's garrisons by his own arms, without much help or hindrance from the Belgians. It is clear that by this time they had little enough enthusiasm for the French—how little may be inferred from the fact that Napoleon was joined by less than 400 of them (out of all his Belgian veterans) in the Hundred Days after his return from Elba. But they had equally little enthusiasm for the Allies; and therein events justified them.

The statesmen who re-mapped Europe were firm against granting Belgium independence, fearing that it would mean its reabsorption by France. The only question which they discussed was, whether the country should be given back to Austria or added to Holland. The Belgians themselves, partly for religious reasons, partly from old ties with the Habsburgs, and partly from that long-developed antipathy towards the Dutch to which we called attention in Chapter III, pleaded for their return to Austria. There was no Belgian party desirous of union with Holland. But Austria did not much want a possession to which she had no longer a land access; and both Prussia and England, especially the Duke of Wellington, advocated the aggrandisement of Holland as a military bulwark against France. Accordingly on July 31, 1814, the Belgian provinces were formally handed over to the Prince of Orange, whom the Dutch had made their Prince-Sovereign the year before. The arrangement was confirmed by the Congress of Vienna, and made to include Liège and Luxemburg; but local discontent was so acute, especially among the Belgian clergy, that there might have been a rising but for Napoleon's escape from Elba. This led to the occupation of Belgium by large bodies of British and German troops; and the events of 1815 preceding and following the battle of Waterloo removed the opportunity for a Belgian popular movement.

The new Prince-Sovereign was proclaimed King William I of the Netherlands in

March 1815. His first business was to raise troops to repel Napoleon. This was done with fair readiness on the part of the population. The Dutch and Belgian regiments were placed under the supreme command of the Duke of Wellington; and both at Quatre Bras and at Waterloo (despite a legend to the contrary long current in England) they fought decidedly well. An ever-memorable addition was made to the long list of historic battles fought on Belgian soil. But when peace was restored, and the union of Belgium and Holland had to be put on a regular footing, the difficulties of the artificial union decreed by the Powers began at once. Holland had in March 1814 adopted a Constitution. It was based on the old Dutch laws and was, among other things, strongly Protestant. A Commission was appointed of eleven Dutch, eleven Belgians, and two representatives for Luxemburg to broaden this into a Constitution of the whole new kingdom. There were long discussions on religion, on the site of the new capital, the form of the new States-General or Parliament, and the number of members which Holland and Belgium should have in it respectively. William I was essentially a Dutch King, and the Dutch felt themselves on the top; but as the Belgians had 50 per cent. more population, a constitution giving them fair representation must have reversed the positions. Eventually the Commission reported in favour of (1) equality and toleration for all creeds throughout the kingdom; (2) a Two-Chamber Parliament in which Holland and Belgium were to have an equal (*i.e.* disproportionate) number of representatives; (3) no capital was specified, but the King was to be inaugurated simultaneously at Amsterdam and at a town in Belgium.

A Fundamental Law was drafted in these terms, and submitted at the same time to the Dutch States-General and the Notables of the different Belgian provinces. The Dutch States-General passed it unanimously. The Belgian Notables rejected it by a large majority. Their rejection was partly, though not wholly, due to unwillingness to legalise religious toleration—the motive which had caused the Brabant Revolution, and which was now fiercely championed by the Bishop of Ghent. William I decided to get over this hostile vote by " cooking " it. He announced that all who had abstained from voting should be counted as voting for the Law, and that a number of the votes against it should not count. In this way he made a sham majority which deceived nobody; and the law was declared passed. On September 21, 1815, he was formally inaugurated as King at

Brussels. A Cabinet was constituted, consisting of nine Dutchmen and one Belgian; and also the new Legislature—an Upper Chamber of life-peers nominated by the King, and a Lower Chamber of 110 members (55 from each country) elected for three years by the Provincial Councils. But the Bishops were unsubdued. They forbade their flocks to take the oath, and thus put all who became members of either Chamber under their ban. This ban was sensationally enforced, until it was successfully defied by the ex-Prince-Bishop of Liége, who, after joining the Upper Chamber, got the Pope on his side and became Archbishop of Malines. The King was then emboldened to use coercion; the Bishop of Ghent was prosecuted, fled the country, and was condemned and deposed in his absence; and for a time the agitation died down.

But the tendency of the Dutch to treat the Belgians as inferiors remained, and was given effect by the Dutch King. Benjamin Constant said a few years after the Union, that of those holding the foremost offices in the kingdom, military or civil, 139 were Dutch and only 30 Belgians. This would have mattered less, had the Belgians been traditionally in the habit of looking up to the Dutch; but the reverse was the case. They knew

themselves more numerous, and thought
themselves culturally superior. After 1820,
the Belgian discontent began to be focussed
in the representative Chamber, where the
eloquence at the command of the Belgian
Opposition was very superior to that of the
Dutch Government. The latter, it should be
noted, was not strictly parliamentary, but
was an emanation from the King, who dis-
owned the doctrines of Ministerial responsi-
bility, and had them carefully kept out of the
Constitution. In this way the situation got
steadily worse, until in 1830 the breach came.

Before we examine this in our next chapter,
and follow out the establishment of Belgian
independence, let us briefly resume the
conclusions which were to be drawn from
Belgium's 365 years' experience of foreign
domination. History had performed on her
a remarkably exhaustive series of experi-
ments. It had first made trial of her protection by, and subjection to, distant non-
contiguous Powers—the two greatest of their
periods, as it happened, Spain and Austria.
The protection had proved definitely inade-
quate—she became the " cockpit of Europe " ;
and the subjection had proved definitely
oppressive—Philip II might be an historical
accident, but the more regular drawbacks of
Spanish and Austrian rule were not so. Follow-

ing these two failures, a strange symmetry of fate subjected her in turn to the two contiguous Powers, first her large neighbour, France, and then her small neighbour, Holland. Here the protection was undoubtedly more efficient; and the subjection, though galling, might in either case have disappeared in time by a process of national amalgamation; only that process would have effaced from the life of Europe one of its rich blooms of national individuality, the ancient and long-developed nationality of the Belgian people. Partly because that nationality was so tenaciously held and passionately treasured by those who possessed it, it did not succumb; indeed, through all the stages of alien rule and oppression one many trace its unity and distinction steadily growing. It was the Spaniards who really made Flanders and Brabant one; it was later, under them and under the Austrians, that Hainaut became no less integral a part of the whole; it was the French who completed Belgium by destroying the separateness of Liége. And so in 1830 History inaugurated her last great experiment; she set the Belgians finally on their own feet to live their lives as an independent nation.

CHAPTER VI

THE ESTABLISHMENT OF BELGIAN
INDEPENDENCE

On the evening of August 25, 1830, the
Brussels Opera House gave a performance of
Auber's *La Muette de Portici*. When the hero
in the piece sang the famous air appealing for
revolt and liberty, the audience were so moved
that they rushed into the streets, looted the
gunsmiths' shops, and started a revolution
against the Dutch then and there. The fire
thus kindled was never put out until it had
consumed all the traces of Belgium's long
subjection, and left her an independent
sovereign state.

Revolutions, says Aristotle, arise on slight
occasions, but not from slight causes. The
discontent in Belgium had grown steadily for
half a generation. It had two roots—the
personal follies and tyrannies of the Dutch
King, William I, and the national inequality
between the Dutch and Belgian peoples. In
1830 the Belgians in round figures numbered

3,900,000 (not the population of what is now Belgium, but of what was then considered Belgium, including the whole of Limburg and Luxemburg), the Dutch 2,300,000. Yet out of eight Ministers of State only one was a Belgian; out of 219 higher officials at the Ministries of the Interior and of War only fourteen were Belgians; and there were only 288 Belgians among the 1967 officers of the army. The ordinance of 1822, making Dutch the sole official language (though till then the speeches in the combined Parliament were almost all made in French), disqualified the whole Walloon population from official employment. It annoyed the Flemings scarcely less, because, although Flemish and Dutch are written alike, the difference of pronunciation made the one unintelligible to an illiterate speaker of the other. Further, by a set of educational measures William I aimed at controlling not only the education of lay people, but that of the Roman Catholic clergy. He, a Protestant, dared repeat almost the very programme which had brought the Catholic Joseph II, with all his Imperial authority and Papal sanction, to grief. Lastly a series of political trials—those of Vanderstraeten in 1819 and 1823, that of Hennequin in 1821, those of Ducpétiaux and De Potter in 1828, and those of De Potter, Tielemans, and

Bartels in 1830—had thrown into sharp relief the despotism of the King and the people's sympathy with those who agitated against it. In October 1829, when the last session of the States-General of the United Netherlands was opened, a National Petition of the Belgian people for the redress of their grievances was laid before it, bearing the signatures of 150,000 heads of families, *i. e.* of practically all who could sign their names. The list included equally Catholics and Liberals, Flemings and Walloons, the representatives of the oldest Belgian noble families, and the rising leaders of the modern movement.

Just as the Brabant Revolution of 1789 took fire from events in Paris and the fall of the Bastille, so the July days, which overthrew the French Legitimist monarchy in 1830, gave the final impulse to the Belgians in August. Belgium was not the only country in Europe which caught the infection of that first uprising against the bonds forged by the Congress of Vienna; but it was the only one whose revolt was a permanent success.

The Brussels revolutionists of August 25, after attacking the houses of unpopular Dutchmen and colliding with the Dutch garrison of the upper town, retired to the lower town, which they held. A Committee of Regency was established in the Hôtel de

Ville. The French tricolor, which had first been hoisted, was replaced by the old Brabant tricolor, which is now the Belgian flag. The other chief towns followed suit, and cooped their Dutch garrisons within the citadels and forts. Some weeks of negotiation followed, during which the Dutch collected troops and the Belgians drilled volunteers. The idea of the Committee of Regency was to secure a separate administration for the Belgian provinces under the Prince of Orange (the King's heir) as Viceroy. The Prince visited Brussels on September 1; and had he shown the requisite tact and insight, he could have secured this solution. But he did not. Things went from bad to worse, and regular hostilities against the rebels became inevitable.

On September 23 a Dutch army nearly 10,000 strong, with many guns, under Prince Frederick, the King's younger son, attacked Brussels. The town then still had its walls and gates. The Dutch assaulted three of the latter, whose sites are still familiar points in its topography. They were repulsed at the Porte de Flandres; but carried the Porte de Schaerbeek and the Porte de Louvain by storm. Their main force entered by the first of these, and swept along the Rue Royale to the park, which lay, as it still lies, in front of the royal palace. The other force from the

Porte de Louvain established itself in the boulevard not far from the Porte de Namur. They thus held the very heart of the upper town; but they could hold no more, because the Belgian volunteers resisted their further progress with desperation. The approach to the Place Royale was defended by a strong barricade with a cannon, and other barricades blocked all the streets leading to the lower town. The windows of the houses round the park and the roof of the Hôtel Bellevue were manned by Belgian sharp-shooters. On the revolutionary side the combatants were merely Brussels citizens, reinforced notably by a band of 300 volunteers brought from Liége by Charles Rogier, by 200 (with the poet-actor Jenneval, author of the "Brabançonne") from Louvain, and by others from various Walloon towns. Nevertheless they sustained the unequal combat in the streets for three days. Every attempt by the Dutch troops to make progress either from the park or from the boulevard was repulsed; and the perpetual sniping to which they were subjected caused them heavy losses. Finally on the night of September 26–27 Prince Frederick, having at least 1500 killed and a very much larger number wounded, evacuated his positions and marched away from the city with his whole force, a defeated man.

This historic street-fight proved the turning-point in the revolution. The records of barricade fighting in the European capitals during the nineteenth century show no other instance in which the success of citizen volunteers over regular troops was so marked, or entailed such important results. The Dutch, though no doubt badly led, were veteran soldiers. The Belgians lost some 600 killed, who were buried in the Place des Martyrs, ever since marked by a well-known monument. With this price they were freed. Their capital was never attacked by the Dutch again.

It would take us too long to trace in detail the events which intervened between this victory and the election of Prince Leopold as King of the Belgians on June 4 in the following year (1831). The first step was to form a Provisional Government. Its members were : Baron d'Hooghvorst, the commander of the volunteers; Charles Rogier of Liége, afterwards Belgian Prime Minister; Count Félix de Mérode, the leader of the Belgian Catholics; Van de Weyer, afterwards Belgian Minister in London and an intimate friend of Queen Victoria; Gendebien, the leader of the French party among the revolutionists; Joly; and De Potter. This Government on

October 4 declared Belgium an independent state, and announced its intention of drafting a Constitution and convening a National Congress to consider and pass it. The Constitution was drafted by a Commission appointed on October 6, which on October 12 decided in favour of a constitutional monarchy. The Congress, which met on November 10, 1830, ratified this decision on November 22. The decree of the Congress, which finally established the Constitution as law, was voted on February 7, 1831.

It has been said with truth of the Belgian revolutionists that after the days of September 23–25 they formed a more adequate conception of their constitutional than of their military tasks. Excellent decrees met all the civil needs of the moment; and the Constitution ultimately evolved has, as we shall see in our next chapter, done great credit to its framers. Unfortunately there was no one to bestow equal care on the military preparations. The Belgians won two small victories over the Dutch in October, and cleared King William's troops out of all the territory then considered Belgium, excepting the citadels of Antwerp, Maestricht, and Luxemburg. But Holland remained a considerable military power; and by neglecting to create

E

a regular army to cope with it, the Belgians exposed themselves to eventual retaliation. In the following year this came about; and though Belgium was saved from reconquest by the attitude of the Powers, and the actual intervention of a French army, she was penalised by losing important territories. These were the portion of Zeeland south of the Schelde, commonly called Dutch Flanders (giving the Dutch complete control over the mouth of that river); a portion of the province of Limburg, including the towns of Maestricht and Venlo; and the portion of Luxemburg, which now forms the Grand Duchy. They were all territories which had joined successfully in the revolt against Holland, and desired incorporation in Belgium.

Already on November 4 a Conference of the Powers to consider the Belgian situation had met in London, and Van de Weyer had been sent there to represent Belgian interests. The Conference tried at once to dictate to the belligerents by means of protocols, which neither the Belgian Congress nor the Dutch King at first welcomed. But in the course of December, on the Belgians proving more amenable than William I, the Conference veered to their side. A protocol of December 20 (carried on the motion of the British dele-

gate, Lord Palmerston) declared Belgium an
" Independent Power." Although this protocol was accepted by neither side (the
Belgians disliked it because it deprived them
of Luxemburg), it marked a definite stage.
Henceforth the question was not whether
Belgium should form a separate kingdom, but
who should be its new King, and what should
be its boundaries.

The position, as it had presented itself to
the Belgian revolutionists, was something like
this. If they set up a Republic (as was the
wish of some, especially De Potter), all the
potentates of Europe, from the Tsar Nicholas I
to the Duke of Wellington, would combine to
crush them. If they attempted the re-
annexation of the country to France (as a
small but active party desired, including
Gendebien, of the Provisional Government,
and Surlet de Chokier, President of the
National Congress), the other four Powers
would make war. They were obliged, therefore, after the hope of a Viceroyalty disappeared, to decide for (a) monarchy; (b)
independence. But much depended on the
choice of the monarch. Two possible candidates came first in the minds of the diplomatists, the Prince of Orange and the Duc de
Nemours, the latter being the younger son of

the new French King, Louis-Philippe. If the Prince of Orange were chosen, Belgium might, at least in regard to its foreign policy, be considered as re-annexed to Holland. If on the other hand the Duc de Nemours were chosen, it might in the same degree be considered as re-annexed to France.

Louis-Philippe was represented at the London Conference by one of the most famous of diplomatists, the veteran Talleyrand. England and Prussia, to whose wish for a buffer against France the union of Holland and Belgium had been due, naturally favoured the candidature of the Prince of Orange. Talleyrand cleverly supported it, knowing that it must fail, and hoping to get the Duc de Nemours finally adopted as the only alternative. On November 24 the Belgian Congress formally excluded all candidatures from the House of Orange-Nassau. On February 3, 1831, after endless intrigues, it decided to offer the crown to the Duc de Nemours. But the Duc only obtained 97 votes out of 192; and partly for this reason, but still more perhaps because the English Ministry resolved unanimously on February 4 to declare war on France if the offer were accepted, King Louis-Philippe declined it on his son's behalf. Intrigues still persisted; Belgian interests continued to suffer; as a makeshift Surlet de Chokier was appointed Regent. It was not till April that his second Ministry approached the Prince Leopold of Saxe-Coburg-Gotha with a tentative offer. On June 4, 1831, the Prince was elected by the National Congress; and on June 21 he was solemnly inaugurated at Brussels as King of the Belgians.

For the final settlement of its international status, the country owed much to Leopold I. Here we may note that he was forty years of age, and had for fifteen years been looked upon as an English prince, in virtue of his marriage in 1816 to Princess Charlotte, the heir to the British throne. Before this marriage he had shown both military and diplomatic ability; and he was regarded by many, including Napoleon, as the handsomest prince of his time. After the Princess Charlotte's death in 1817, the Prince, enjoying an English pension of £50,000 a year and residing at Claremont, was a conspicuous figure at the court of his father-in-law. He arranged the marriage of his sister with the Duke of Kent; and when the Duke died leaving the Duchess and her young daughter (afterwards Queen Victoria) almost totally unprovided for, the Prince took them into his house, which for

many years was the future Queen's home.
In 1830 he was a candidate for the throne of
Greece, but declined at the last moment, as
he could not get from the Powers what he
thought sufficiently good terms. It was
probably due to this circumstance that his
name was not put forward earlier for the
throne of Belgium, as his person was well
regarded by all the courts except Berlin and
Paris. He eventually won over the latter
by promising to marry (as he subsequently
did) Louis-Philippe's daughter, the Princess
Louise. By this marriage of a French princess
to a quasi-English prince the conflict of French
and English interests in Belgium appeared to
be neutralised.

The Prince's first business, before finally
accepting the throne, was to get the question
of Belgian territory settled to the satisfaction
of his future subjects. The London Conference had issued two protocols on January 20
and 27, which laid down (1) that Belgium
should be a perpetually neutral state; (2) that
the territories of Holland should be all which
belonged to the Dutch Republic in 1790, and
the Grand Duchy of Luxemburg should also
be an appanage of the House of Orange;
(3) that Belgium should be charged with
16/31 of the National Debt of the now divided

kingdom. These protocols were accepted by King William, but refused by the Belgians. They did not desire any of the three points which we have mentioned; but their great objection was to the second. Its effect was to rob them of " Dutch Flanders " (which controlled the Schelde), of the towns Maestricht and Venlo and the strip of Limburg surrounding them, and also of the Grand Duchy—deprivations which seemed the harder, because by their own arms and with the concurrence of the inhabitants they had expelled the Dutch from the whole of these areas, excepting the citadels of Maestricht and Luxemburg. When the Prince intervened there was a complete deadlock between the Powers and the Belgians on these points. Leopold skilfully disposed of it by persuading the London Conference to supersede its protocols by a declaration in Eighteen Articles, whereby the matter in dispute and other possible bargains between Belgium and Holland were left open to be negotiated between the new King and King William with the good offices of the Great Powers. After this considerable diplomatic victory the Prince was received by the Belgians with enthusiasm, and took over the monarchy.

But his first success was short-lived. The

removal of the territorial decision from the London Conference to the two states primarily concerned would have benefited Belgium had she kept herself on a military equality with Holland. But she had not. What was left of the volunteer armies that had expelled the Dutch had during these months of intrigue and delay sunk to the lowest depths of inefficiency. King William, on the other hand, had spent the year consolidating his army. He refused to recognise the Eighteen Articles, declared the armistice at an end, and on August 2, twelve days after Leopold had ascended the throne, he invaded Belgium. In this difficult situation Leopold I displayed both military ability and personal courage, but his defeat was inevitable. The Belgians fought bravely, but were entirely outnumbered. On the breaking-off of the armistice the King had promptly appealed for the assistance of a French army; and this fortunately arrived before the Dutch had taken Brussels, though not till they had taken Louvain. The Dutch then retired from Belgium; but their object was accomplished: the Eighteen Articles were dead.

The promptitude and success of the French intervention alarmed the other Powers, especially England, and revived their Dutch

sympathies. On October 15 a protocol of
Twenty-four Articles was drafted in place
of the eighteen, which took from Belgium
the whole of the areas in dispute, except the
district of Arlon. Under threat of invasion
by a German army the Belgians were forced
to accept this ; and on November 15 Belgium,
France, and England signed a treaty incorpor-
ating the articles, to which Russia, Prussia,
and Austria soon afterwards adhered. But
Holland still stood out. King William refused to evacuate the points which he held,
especially the citadel of Antwerp. In
December a French Army advanced for the
second time, and captured this citadel after
a brave defence by the Dutch general, Chassé ;
but other Belgian positions remained in Dutch
hands, and the Belgians in return declined to
evacuate the areas of Limburg and Luxemburg assigned to King William. A Conven-
tion signed in May 1832 brought about a
temporary armistice on this footing. So the
affair dragged on for nearly six years, till in
1838 King William suddenly gave his adhesion
to the 1831 treaty. The Conference of
London met again to see what changes, if
any, were rendered advisable by lapse of
time. King Leopold secured for Belgium a
large reduction in its payment to the Nether-

E 2

lands Debt; but he failed to get territorial changes. The final treaty was signed in London on April 18, 1839, when the disputed areas, which the Belgians had held for over eight years, were very reluctantly surrendered.

The treaty of 1839, which unlike that of 1831 was ratified by all the Governments concerned, regulated the external position of Belgium down to August 3, 1914. It is the " scrap of paper," of which so much has been heard since that date. The clause imposing perpetual neutrality on Belgium with the guarantee of the five Great Powers was taken over from the treaty of 1831. It had been imposed on her against her will, at the instance chiefly of Prussia and England, who desired above all to maintain her as a bulwark against France. There is an interesting passage in Queen Victoria's Letters on this point. The Queen writes (February 12, 1856) to Leopold I—

> Belgium of its own accord bound itself to remain neutral, and its very existence is based upon that neutrality, which the other Powers have guaranteed and are bound to maintain if Belgium keeps her engagements.

The King promptly replies (February 15, 1856)—

This neutrality was in the real interest of this country, but our good Congress here did *not* wish it; it was *imposé* upon them.

Historically the King was right, and it is probable that but for this compulsion Belgium would have come into the French orbit. France was the only Power which wished in the first instance to see her liberated from Holland; and while this desire was in part motived by natural sympathy between the Parisian and Belgian revolutionists, what weighed more with Louis-Philippe and Talleyrand was the hope of reacquiring the strategic control over the Low Countries, which had been enjoyed by Napoleon.

The only time during eighty-three years at which it seemed seriously threatened was in 1870. As early as 1852, on the morrow of his *Coup d'État*, Napoleon III (then the Prince-President of France) signed a decree annexing Belgium; but he withdrew it before publication at the instance of the Duc de Morny. The rise of Prussia in the 'sixties, following that of France in the 'fifties, revived a possibility that Belgium might be fought over or partitioned or bargained away between her great neighbours. Indeed in 1870 Bismarck published a draft treaty, three or

four years old, and in the handwriting of
Napoleon III's ambassador, whereby France
was to annex her. This publication, on the eve
of the Franco-German hostilities, so alarmed
the British Government that it at once increased its army and invited Paris and Berlin
to sign short treaties reaffirming the neutrality
clause of 1839. Bismarck promptly assented;
for the neutrality of Belgium seemed then,
as it always had, to be an anti-French, not a
French interest; and the assent of Napoleon
III's Government followed later. One should
note that the treaties of 1870 in no way
superseded that of 1839; on the contrary,
they strengthened it, by showing in a test
case that both the contiguous Powers would
respect its principle, and England would
enforce such respect. After Sedan no further
risk of its violation appeared till early in the
twentieth century, when the construction by
Prussia of strategic railways towards the
Belgian frontier first presaged the storm which
broke in 1914.

The Belgians, though at first undesirous of
neutrality, have long come to value it as the
best safeguard against their again becoming
the " cockpit of Europe." The expansion of
their foreign ambitions in recent years, and the
annexation of an African Empire eighty-fold

larger than their European territory, have not altered this sentiment. The policy of their Kings and of their wisest statesmen has been to keep alive the guarantee of the Powers, and at the same time to build up such means of defence as would either deter any possible aggressor, or at least make an example of him sufficient to deter others. Whether the Belgian resistance of 1914, heroic as it was, has sufficed for this purpose, it remains for history to show. It would have been more effective but for two causes: one, the long resistance of a Germanophile wing within the Catholic party (led by M. Woeste) to the strengthening of the army; the other an excessive reliance on forts. To the first it was due that the first modern law which gave Belgium an army at all corresponding to her population was only passed in 1913, and its effects were only beginning to be felt when war broke out. The reliance on fortresses was doubtless well advised twenty, or perhaps ten years ago; but unfortunately the development of modern artillery had made them out of date by the time that their efficacy was put to the test.

CHAPTER VII

THE BELGIAN CONSTITUTION

THE Belgian Constitution has been often and justly admired. It is the oldest written Constitution still in force on the Continent, except the Dutch; and has not, like the latter, been modified past recognition. The success of its authors was due to the fact that they reduced fancy innovations to a minimum, and built as far as possible on existing bases. These bases were the charters and privileges of the different Belgian provinces and cities, which dated from the Middle Ages, and had been carefully conserved, however often infringed, throughout the long episodes of Spanish and Austrian oppression. The most important for modern purposes was the Joyous Entry of Duke Wenceslas of Brabant (1356), which in the Austrian period, with the steady preponderance of Brabant as the metropolitan province, came to be regarded as something like the Magna Charta of the whole country. We have already seen how the clerical agitators who brought about the Brabant Revolution in 1789 took their stand on certain of its provisions. These provisions, which were held to preclude toleration for other religions than the Roman Catholic, were among the few which were drastically superseded and swept away by the Constitution of 1831.

On the top of the Joyous Entry the Belgian Constitution-makers erected a system of constitutional monarchy modelled on the England of their day and the France of Louis Philippe. The machinery which they established, of a King, a Senate, and a Chamber of Representatives, has only provoked revolutionary discontent or required fundamental change in respect of a single feature, the franchise. Very noticeable is the organic relation which was, and is still, preserved between the central power of the State and the local councils of the provinces; which in their modern form still represent, with no great breach of historic continuity, the provincial States-General, that came down from the later Burgundian times.

The legislative power is wielded by the King, the Chamber, and the Senate collectively. The initiative in legislation may be taken by any of the three; but laws regarding finance or the annual contingent for the army must first be voted by the Chamber. Legislation may not contravene the Constitution, but is otherwise unlimited in scope. Changes of the Constitution can only be effected by a special procedure. First the two Chambers must pass a resolution, declaring that there is reason for changing a particular article in the Constitution. By this vote both are *ipso facto* completely dissolved, and a new Parliament must be elected; which thereupon has the right to change, if it pleases, the article in question. But the change cannot be discussed without a quorum of two-thirds, nor carried without a two-thirds majority of those present.

Ministers have a right of access to both Chambers; and either can demand their presence. They are entitled to be heard on demand. A Minister may not, however, vote or participate informally in a discussion, unless he is otherwise a member of the particular Chamber concerned. The sittings of both Chambers are public, and members and senators are immune from prosecution for votes or speeches.

The executive power is vested in the Crown, which, as in England, can only act through responsible Ministers. All the King's acts must be countersigned by a Minister who makes himself responsible thereby. The number of Ministries is now eleven. They are: (1) War; (2) Interior; (3) Finance; (4) Foreign Affairs; (5) Science and Art; (6) Justice; (7) Agriculture and Public Works; (8) Railways; (9) Marine, Posts, and Telegraphs; (10) Industry and Labour; (11) Colonies. The last has only existed since 1908, when the independent Congo Free State (of which the then King of the Belgians, Leopold II, was sovereign) was transferred to Belgium as a colony; and some of the others are, as separate Ministries, of even more recent origin. The Cabinet may, as is usual on the Continent, include other Ministers without portfolios.

The franchise set up for the Chamber in 1831 was an extremely narrow one, based on the amount paid by each citizen in taxation. The urban electorate, composed of men paying seventy florins in taxes, was particularly unrepresentative. In 1848 the Liberal Ministry reduced the qualification to twenty florins (they could reduce it thus far, but not further, without changing the text of the Constitution), and on this still very narrow basis all elections were held down to 1894. On October 14 in that year the first election was held on the present basis, which gives at least one vote to every male citizen who has attained the age of twenty-five and been domiciled one year in the same commune (the commune is the smallest area of local government). The consequence in 1894 was to increase the number of voters from 137,772 to 1,350,891; but its effect was and is considerably modified by the simultaneous grant of additional votes to certain of the electors. This so-called plural-voting system gives one additional vote to every father of a family, aged 35 or more, who pays 5 francs in direct taxes, and to every man over 25 drawing 100 francs income from Belgian funds or owning land with a cadastral revenue of 48 francs. The " cadastral revenue " is an assessment of land (including buildings), on which the land-tax is levied; it was made in 1858, on the basis of the actual letting value during the previous decade and has not been altered since. Two other extra votes are given to holders of certain diplomas and certificates of learning and to members of certain professions; but no one can cast more than three votes altogether. As a result, the 1,350,891 voters of 1894 cast 2,085,605 votes. The plural voting system is so important a matter of controversy in modern Belgium that it is necessary to form a clear arithmetical idea of it. This may be obtained from the adjoining table, showing for the year of registration 1912–1913 the number of electors and the number of plural votes for both the Senate and the Chamber.

	Senate.	Chamber.
No. of voters . . .	1,483,994	1,745,666
No. with 1 vote . . .	761,864	1,005,094
No. with 2 votes . .	402,444	412,721
No. with 3 votes . .	319,686	327,351
Total number of votes .	2,525,810	2,814,089
Excess of votes over voters	1,941,816	1,068,423
Excess per cent. . .	70	61

It will be noticed that the plural voter wields more power over the Senate than over the Chamber. The reason for this is the absence of young voters from the Senatorial electorate; its result is to help make the Senate the more conservative body. Even in the case of the Chamber the effect of the system must be very great. It will be seen that on the above figures the propertyless class of manual workers, who have but one vote apiece, were nearly 59 per cent. of the voters, but had less than 36 per cent. of the voting power; in other words, they were reduced from a decisive majority to a weak minority. The system particularly favours the numerous clergy, both secular and regular, and the small landowners in the peasant districts; and for these reasons is generally thought to have been of most advantage to the Catholic party. The class most handicapped by it is that of the workmen in the towns; and it is the party most dependent on them, the Socialists, who have led the agitation for sweeping the plural votes away.

There are twenty-nine large constituencies for the Chamber; and each member must represent a quota of not less than 40,000 inhabitants. For the directly elected portion of the Senate there are twenty-one large constituencies; and each of the elected Senators must represent not less than 80,000. The Senatorial electorate differs from that for the Chamber in that it is confined to voters aged thirty years and upwards. An additional contingent of Senators is that separately elected by the Councils of the provinces; which are each entitled to appoint two Senators if their population is less than half a million, three if it exceeds half a million, and four if it exceeds one million. The Senate is therefore a composite body, chosen partly by an electorate from which the younger voters for the Chamber are excluded, and partly by the

Provincial Councils. It contains no hereditary members except the sons, or the heir-
apparent, of a king; who acquire membership at eighteen, and the right to vote at
twenty-five. We should add, that every
elector qualified to vote is also compelled by
law under penalty to do so; that voting
takes place in the communes, whose Burgomasters and *Échevins* annually revise the
lists; that the constituencies polled are all
polled on the same day; that the ballot is
secret; and that elections are very rarely
disputed or invalidated.

By a law of December 29, 1899, the Constitution was further modified in order to
establish a system of Proportional Representation. Belgium was the first country in
Europe to adopt Proportional Representation
of any kind. The system chosen was one invented by the late Prof. D'Hondt of Ghent,
and may be termed the " party list " system.
It assumes the existence of organised parties;
and provides facilities for each party to put
forward, in the large constituencies which are
part of the plan, not merely isolated candidates, but lists of candidates arranged in
the party's order of preference. There are
no by-elections; each party provides for
possible vacancies by dividing its list

into two sections known as "titular" and "supplementary" candidates. The vote is recorded not by making a cross, as in England, but by blacking out a white spot in the centre of a black square. Such a square stands on the ballot paper at the head of every party list, and also beside every individual name. The elector has four alternatives. He may—

(1) Black the square at the head of his party list. In this case he votes for the whole list and its order.

(2) Black the square beside the name of a "supplementary" candidate. Here he votes for the whole list, but for modifying the order of the "supplementary" candidates in favour of the one blacked.

(3) Black the square beside the name of a "titular" candidate. Here he votes for the whole list, but modifying the order of the "titular" candidates in favour of the one blacked.

(4) Combine the last two operations by blacking the squares beside the name of one "titular" and one "supplementary" candidate.

From this it may be seen that the individual elector has but little escape from the choices of his party. Suppose, for instance, his party puts forward a list of four candidates: A,

B, C, D, and he considers one of them, say B, to be an undesirable scoundrel. He has no means of not voting for him, short of abandoning A, C, D, and his party ticket altogether; though by blacking the square opposite C or D he can vote for moving B one place down in the order of preference. Experience shows that nearly all electors are content to black the square at the head of the list, and thus adopt their party's decision in its entirety. Herein they are little better or worse off than electors under the systems current in England and America; though the second ballot system, which prevails in France and Italy and for the German Reichstag, undoubtedly gives the individual elector, for good or evil, more choice regarding the individual who is to represent him.

When the votes have been recorded, the next step is to allot the seats. How this is done can best be shown by an example. Suppose an election for five seats, and suppose four party lists obtain 24,000, 11,000, 9000 and 3000 votes respectively. These figures are then divided by two, with results 12,000, 5500, 4500, 1500; by three, with results 8000, 3660, 3000, 1000; and then if necessary by four, and so on. As there are five seats, the fifth largest of the figures thus obtained (in this case the figure 8000) will be the " quotient "; and by dividing it into the original figures 24,000, 11,000, 9000 and 3000 we shall find the number of seats obtained by each party. Consequently they will be 3, 1, 1, and 0 respectively.

This system of Proportional Representation having now been over fifteen years in force, and having been exemplified every two years during that period, one can draw certain conclusions regarding it with tolerable certainty. In the first place its effect is distinctly conservative. No party can increase or diminish its number of seats save by very slow processes of growth and attrition; and political landslides, as we know them in Great Britain and the United States, are quite out of the question. Secondly, although the results yielded are much more " proportional " on the whole than those under the oldest electoral systems, it still gives a disproportionate advantage to the big battalions. If two parties of equal size combine their forces and run a single ticket, they will tend to get more than twice the number of seats that would have fallen to them separately. Consequently the history of Belgian parties, since Proportional Representation was introduced, has been one of fusion and consolidation. The first victim of this tendency after 1899 was, curiously enough, the little party which had most favoured the reform, viz. the so-called Independent party led by M. Théodor, consisting of Conservatives who were not Clericals. They were almost immediately submerged and their forces gathered back into the Conservative-Clerical fold. Similarly the Liberal party before 1899 had practically been split into two between the Old Liberals or *Doctrinaires,* under various leaders, and the *Progressistes* or Radicals, led by the brilliant and eloquent M. Paul Janson. But Proportional Representation speedily reconverted them into a single political host; and in 1914, under the leadership of M. Paul Hymans, the combined Belgian Liberal party was at least as united as it has ever been. The same tendency even operated at the 1912 elections to effect a partial alliance between the Liberals and the Socialists; and in Flanders, where both of them are weakest, such a " cartel " between them for election purposes has long been a favourite idea of their local politicians, however much frowned on by their less compromising leaders elsewhere. But not the least striking example is provided by the dominant Catholic party itself. This party, which has held office for thirty years, includes extremely divergent schools within its ranks. There have always been broadly two sections, one of which is Conservative first and Catholic afterwards, another which is Catholic first and only Conservative, if at all, so far as Conservative support is indispensable for the maintenance of Catholic interests. But each section contains its sub-sections; and the divergencies between the extreme wings of both have grown so great that nothing but the mechanical pressure of the electoral system could keep them longer together. Before 1899 the extremest democrats of the party had already broken off, under the leadership of a socialistic priest, the late Abbé Dæns, and had formed a separate organisation, the Christian Democrats; who, though visited with the displeasure of the Belgian episcopate, grew fast in such Flemish centres as Alost, and seemed likely to have a future. After 1899 the cold blasts of Proportional Representation speedily curtailed their prospects.

The Deputies are paid 4000 francs (£160), and given free railway passes to travel between their homes and Parliament. Senators are unpaid. Any one who possesses a vote for the Chamber is also eligible for it. Candi-

dates for the Senate require a stiffer qualification; they must be at least forty years of
age, and pay £48 in direct taxes, or own land
of £480 cadastral revenue. The Chamber is
renewed by halves every two years (failing
a dissolution); the Senate, by halves every
four years. This does not mean that every
constituency votes biennially to elect half its
members; but that the constituencies of the
country are divided into two groups, of which
one elects its members on any given biennial
occasion, and the other on the occasion following. These are called " partial " elections.
Though the practice thus differs in detail
from that of English municipal councils, whose
membership is elected annually by thirds, it
is similar in so far as it preserves a large
element of continuity in the composition of
the Chambers. It reinforces the conservative tendency, which we have noted as a
consequence of Proportional Representation.
A dissolution of Parliament, in the English
sense, is a very rare event. In practice it
may occur in two cases: (1) in the course
of the procedure described above for amending an article in the Constitution both
Chambers are completely dissolved; (2) where
a partial election has reduced the Government's majority too low for it to remain in

office, without giving an actual majority to the other side, the King, who has always a right of dissolving either or both Chambers, will dissolve them to clear up the position. This was done by Leopold II in 1870; but the necessity for it cannot often arise.

The main areas of local government are the province and the commune. Within the nine provinces there are over 2600 communes. Each province has a Governor, an elected Council and a " permanent deputation." The Governor is the nominee of the central government. His duty is to preserve order and as head of the provincial administration to preside over the permanent deputation, participating thus in the management of provincial affairs and in the control which the deputation exercises over those of the communes.

The Provincial Council is elected by the same voters as the Senate. It is, however, elected by an ordinary majority vote, and the councillors need not be more than twenty-five years of age. They hold office for eight years, and their membership is renewed by halves quadrennially. The Council does not meet very often, its detailed day-to-day business being carried on by the " permanent deputation." The " permanent deputation " consists of six members who hold office for eight years. Every four years the Council elects three of their number. The deputation is the regular organ of the Council for : (a) administering the affairs of the province; (b) exercising a control over the finance and administration of the communes. It is quite an old institution, which was already flourishing in Austrian times. Communes with less than 5000 inhabitants are grouped in *arrondissements,* for each of whom there is appointed a Commissioner (*commissaire*) whose duty it is to supervise their administration under the direction of the Governor and the " permanent deputation."

The larger communes with over 5000 population have an autonomy of their own, many of whose features descend from the Middle Ages. The Communal Council is elected by the same voters as the Senate; save that the voter must have been domiciled three years in the commune, and can have extra votes in virtue of paying a certain amount of taxes (which varies according to the population of the commune), or owning land of a certain cadastral revenue. The maximum number of votes which any elector may cast is four. The Councillors must be at least twenty-five years of age, and live in the commune. They are not elected by wards, but by proportional representation under a system somewhat different from that in force for the Parliament. There are also supplementary Councillors representing capital and labour, of whom half are elected by employers and half by employees; the electorates being those which elect certain statutory " Councils of Industry and Labour," whose business it is to avert and mitigate labour disputes. In a commune where the population is between 20,000 and 70,000, there are four of these supplementary Councillors; in larger communes there are eight. Councillors hold their seats for eight years, half their number being elected at quadrennial intervals. In each commune a " college," consisting of a Burgomaster and *Échevins*, is elected by the Council from its members. Strictly speaking, the Council only selects the Burgomaster; the King appoints him; and the royal approval, though usually given, is not a matter of course—*e. g.* Leopold II always refused to appoint a Socialist. The Burgomaster holds office for ten years, and is personally responsible for the police. The nearest British equivalent to the *Échevins* are aldermen in England, and bailies in Scotland; the French and German equivalents are much nearer. But the constitution of the Belgian municipalities, though it bears the marks of Napoleon's reorganising genius, is not the pure Napoleonic type found in France and West Germany. The French and West German mayors are autocrats; the " adjoints," who correspond to the *Échevins*, are little more than their servants; the Council's functions are chiefly consultative. In Belgium both *Échevins* and Council have more power. The " college" above described is a joint executive more like the *Magistrat* of an East German municipality; and the Council itself has also executive functions. For instance, whereas in France and West Germany the Mayor appoints the municipal servants, in Belgium their appointments are made by the whole Council. The *Échevins* number from two to four according to the population of the town; and in certain great towns there are five of them. The functions of the " college " which they form with the Burgomaster fall under two main heads : (1) it is the agent of the Council to carry out its resolutions; (2) it is the agent of the Central Government to keep the electoral registers and enforce the laws and decrees.

The titles " Burgomaster " and " *Échevin* " go back to the twelfth and thirteenth centuries. The first step in the freeing of the

Flemish communes from feudalism was the
appointment of *Échevins* to rule them. These
officials were selected by the Count of Flanders,
but they were members of the citizen body.
Before the year 1200, in some cases, the communes obtained the further right of appointing what were called Juries (*jurés*). These
bodies (whose membership varied in number
in the different towns) consisted of sworn
representatives elected by the Guilds (*Métiers*)
to represent them and to try all cases affecting their members. They came to form in
effect a Town Council, and to appoint one
(or sometimes two) of their number to act as
Burgomaster, *i. e.* head of the burghers.
There was originally, therefore, a certain
opposition between the Burgomaster, who
represented the civic electorate, and the
Échevins, who were the nominees of the
Count. The office of *Échevin* early became
hereditary in certain patrician families; and
it was these who formed the backbone of the
Leliaerts and similar factions, which sided
with the Counts of Flanders and the French
monarchy against the popular parties in the
great cities. The great popular leader, Jacobus
Van Artevelde, as we have seen (Chapter III),
was a member of this class; but he was the
exception. The process by which the Burgomaster and *Échevins* have been formed into

a single college appointed by the Communal Council to act as its executive was accomplished by stages, which we have not time to trace here. But the antiquity and continuous tradition associated with the titles borne by these modern functionaries undoubtedly increases the strong hold which they have on the popular imagination in Belgium. The Burgomasters of the four great towns, Brussels, Antwerp, Liége and Ghent, loom very large in the nation's public life; and more than once in constitutional crises, when Parliament itself seemed unable to settle national problems, they have (as in 1899 and again in 1913), intervened collectively with great moral authority.

The financial systems prescribed for the State and municipalities are such as to secure effective public control. The State taxes are voted annually, and laws imposing them must be annually renewed. Every year before the budget of receipts and expenditure is brought before the Chambers it has to be submitted to the examination of the *Cour des Comptes* or Board of Audit, a body of eight auditors appointed by the Chamber of Deputies. The Board's duty is to see that the sums granted by Parliament have not been exceeded, and amounts voted for one purpose have not been spent on another. The Provincial and Com-

F

munal Councils must also have annual budgets,
and in each case (save in specified exceptions)
no local tax can be imposed without the con-
sent of the whole Council. The expenditure
of the provinces is under the supervision of
the same *Cour des Comptes* which examines
that of the State. In the communes the
Burgomaster and *Échevins* are directly responsible for the management of expenditure;
and the financial position of the communes
must be checked at least once a quarter.
The approval of the Crown is needed for the
budgets of expenditure of both provinces and
communes; but in the case of the communes
this control is not exercised in such a way as to
restrict substantially the very large autonomy
which it is traditional for them to enjoy.

Such is a brief sketch of the political and
administrative machinery under the Constitution of 1831 as modified during eighty-three
years of rapid national development. Bearing
that development in mind the modifications
do not seem many. But another equally important feature of the Constitution is its
effective guarantee of private rights. The
liberty of the subject is nowhere better
safeguarded than in Belgium. The old Constitutions or "privileges" dating from the
thirteenth and fourteenth centuries were
extremely effective under this head; and if

Belgium became the scene of a most arbitrary tyranny under the Duke of Alva and many more of his Spanish and Austrian successors, it was simply because these foreign rulers, by the aid of their foreign armies, overrode them altogether. As Prof. Pirenne justly points out, they stood the strain even under Philip II until the arrival of Alva with his Spanish regiments enabled all law to be ignored. These "privileges," typically embodied, as we have said, in the Joyous Entry of Brabant, were reaffirmed in 1831 with the necessary modernisations and extensions; and by being enacted in the Constitution have all the peculiar security against violation attaching to the clauses of that Fundamental Law. The following observations delivered in the Belgian Court of Cassation over forty years ago by a very eminent lawyer, the late M. Charles Faider, are as true to-day as they were then—

Freedom reigns among us without flaw and without infringement. It takes every form; it sustains every right. I have freedom of the person; and I can only be arrested in the prescribed manner. I have freedom of the home; and my dwelling is inviolable, subject to the rule of law. I have freedom of property; and I am guaranteed against expropriation, confiscation, and arbitrary taxes, as well as the forfeitures which have been abolished. I have freedom of activity; I am free to work, to choose my trade, to enter into industrial contracts. I have freedom of opinion; for all the channels of the Press and of publication are open to me. I have freedom of speech; for I can speak freely, whether in Parliament, in the pulpit, in the police court, at the Bar, and in whatever language. I have freedom of thought; for no one may violate the privacy of my letters, and the law lays no hand on my thoughts, even my guilty thoughts. I have freedom of worship; for my conscience is free, the ministers of my religion are independent, I may let it exert its full influence and efficacity for me. I have freedom of instruction; for I am allowed to teach and to learn, where I like and at every stage, what is known and what is believed. I have freedom of movement; for every barrier has disappeared within the country, and the protection of foreigners is assured. I am free to seek help, to claim justice, to make my voice heard against any oppression; for I can use when I please the right of petition.

Here I am, therefore, as a citizen, in the peaceable enjoyment of genuine freedom.

To a British subject or an American citizen in the twentieth century these phrases may perhaps seem trite. He may fancy that such elementary liberties are the conditions of civilisation, and ought to be taken for granted. But in point of fact there are many Continental countries in which they still do not exist; and there is not one, except Switzerland, in which they have existed continuously, as in Belgium, for the past eighty-four years. The Belgian judiciary, whose reputation justly stands high, have maintained them without fail; and the existence of this little country, with its free Press, and freedom of the individual from arbitrary arrest, was of incalculable value throughout the middle of last century to the cause of liberty in the countries adjoining it. French, Dutch, and German political refugees found in it their nearest haven and their most convenient base of operations, even though diplomacy sometimes succeeded in restricting the latter use of it. Moreover, the country's own freedom from revolutionary movements during the first fifty years of its separate and independent existence gave, like that of Great Britain, a most valuable advertisement to the cause of liberty, which was thus shown not to be subversive of public order, but its most effective guarantee.

CHAPTER VIII

POLITICS AND PARTIES IN MODERN BELGIUM

THERE have always been in Belgium since 1830 at least two parties, Catholics and Liberals; and all Ministries, before the outbreak of the European War, have represented one of these, or a coalition of the two. The Revolution itself was the product of their co-operation, and for fifteen years after Leopold I's advent the country was governed by coalition Ministries. In 1846 the parties separated. The subsequent alternations of power have been as follows : 1846–7, Catholics; 1847–55, Liberals; 1855–57, Catholics; 1857–70, Liberals; 1870–8, Catholics; 1878–84, Liberals; 1884–1914, Catholics. On the outbreak of war in 1914 the Ministry in power made itself a coalition Ministry by admitting the leaders of the Liberal and Socialist parties.

The division between the Catholic and Liberal parties was and is primarily religious. The Catholic party represents the interests of ecclesiasticism in Belgium; interests of a very complicated kind, since the Roman Church is, through its various organisations,

the largest property-owner in the country.
There is not, and never has been since the
end of the sixteenth century, any but the
one Church. The very small number of
Protestants are practically all foreigners,
and the Jews are numerically negligible. A
Belgian is almost invariably either a Roman
Catholic or a Freethinker; let us add, as a
social and political factor of some consequence,
that a Belgian woman is almost invariably a
Roman Catholic. The last point had has the
curious consequence, that on various occasions, during the recurrent franchise dispute
Catholics have suggested Women's Suffrage,
which Liberals and Socialists have rejected.

The moderate Liberals or *doctrinaires* are
men who attend Mass and remain in com-
munion with the Church, but oppose the
policy of the episcopate and the clergy in
such matters as education or the legal status
of convents. The extremer Liberals correspond to the Radicals and Socialistic-Radicals
in France; they are definitely hostile to
religion. A similar hostility is almost universal among the Belgian Socialists; indeed
the Church, by laying its official ban upon
their ideas and organisation, has left them
practically no alternative.

Behind this predominant cleavage over
Church issues, to which there is no real

parallel in England and none whatever in America (unless perhaps in the State of Utah, where the political position of the Mormon Church presents some analogies to that of Catholicism in Flanders), the more strictly political cleavages are somewhat vague and shifting. The Liberals on the whole have been the party of *laisser-faire*, the party opposed to State intervention and regulation; an attitude which came to them the more easily, because their most influential supporters were the manufacturers and coal-owners of the Walloon provinces. They have also been the Francophile party—sympathetic, that is to France, and upholders in Belgium of the French language. Circumstances have latterly modified their collective views in a more popular direction, but they remain, on the whole, the party of the well-to-do urban classes. So long as the Belgian franchise was a very narrow one they could hold their own against the Catholics in the political see-saw; indeed, out of forty-nine years' party government, they held power during twenty-eight. The widening of the franchise in 1894 was a blow from which they have never yet recovered. The popular masses in Belgium are either (as in the dense Flemish country-side) devotedly religious; or else (as in the Walloon industrial areas) they

want some hotter gospel of democracy than
Belgian Liberalism has supplied.

The Catholic party is not easy to appraise
justly, because it presents so many faces.
The most unpleasant of these perhaps is
its scurrilous gutter Press, which is easily
the most foul-mouthed in Belgium. Its
net effect is less conservative than might be
inferred from the fact that there is no other
Conservative party. There are, of course,
certain matters, on which the Catholic Church
always champions the *status quo* against all
change. Its educational policy, which delayed the establishment of compulsory
education until 1914, cannot be acquitted
of the charge of hampering elementary instruction, and causing the mass of illiteracy
which is so deplorable in the most Catholic
areas. Nevertheless, ever since the first
rebellion of the industrial proletariat in 1886,
some sections of the party have taken a
genuine interest in social, as opposed to
political, reform. The more ardent of those
thus engaged are genuine and valuable social
workers. It is the case that practically
all the social legislation of Belgium has been
enacted by the Catholics, and some of it
has been thoroughly well conceived. The
Catholic organisation has also been the
chief one to occupy itself with the problems of

F 2

the agriculturists and peasants. The agricultural co-operative societies, the Raiffeisen banks and the admirable system of agricultural education, are mainly due to its initiative. That these have been created less for their own sake than in order to weave nets of Church influence over the people, does not alter the fact that they are social boons, and that the priests stationed in every village have proved themselves a uniquely successful agency for organising and carrying them out.

The election of 1894 introduced to the Parliament for the first time the Socialist party. The widened franchise gave it twenty-nine seats right off; and the accession to its ranks and leadership of a remarkable band of intellectually eminent men, concentrated on it an attention which it has never lost. Beginning in 1885 as a Labour Party (*Parti Ouvrier*), composed like the British Labour Party of Socialists, trade unionists, and co-operators in alliance, it has gradually and without serious friction, become a Socialist organisation throughout. But its strength has always lain in its co-operative stores, which form centres of personal attachment, of propaganda, and of revenue, not less powerful in their way, though less ubiquitous, than the Church organisation of the Catholics. Against these potent engines of its rivals the Liberal party can set nothing comparable except the anti-religious freemasons' lodges; which, in spite of much recent development, are an altogether less formidable weapon. No party, however, can claim the monopoly of any such social device. Trade unions, co-operative stores, co-operative agricultural societies, organisations of every kind for pleasure, profit, or social intercourse, tend to be started by all the parties in turn as soon as one has proved their electoral value. The result, as a most careful English observer, Mr. Seebohm Rowntree, has noted, is an unusually deep cleavage between parties throughout the whole social structure. As he says—

There is extraordinarily little social intercourse between Catholics and Liberals, and practically none between Catholics and Socialists. Politics enter into almost every phase of social activity and philanthropic effort, and it is the exception rather than the rule for persons holding different political opinions to co-operate in any other matter. Thus in one town there will be a Catholic, a Liberal, and a Socialist trade union, a Catholic, a Liberal, and a Socialist co-operative bakery, a Catholic, a Liberal, and a Socialist thrift society, each catering for similar people, but each confining its attentions to members of its own political party. The separation extends to cafés, gymnasia, choral, temperance, and literary societies; indeed, it cuts right through life. There is everywhere this division of the social forces, leading to a serious dissipation of power. Moreover, it often happens that one of the parties, in any particular town, is not strong enough to maintain an organisation. In such cases its members must either dispense with its benefits or leave their party in order to enjoy them elsewhere. Such adhesion to a political party through economic pressure tends to political and religious hypocrisy. Social work on a neutral basis, though often tried by independent groups of reformers, has seldom succeeded.

The drawbacks of this cleavage from a national standpoint are obvious. The reason for it is that two of the parties concerned, the Catholics and Socialists, are not merely political, but seek to be the many-sided exponents of a whole way of life, in which politics is only a phase. For this reason even the compelling influence of the war of 1914 seems less likely to break down the exaggeration of party differences than that of some other national cleavages. Nevertheless, the formation, for the first time since 1846, of a Ministry representing all parties cannot but exert a certain assuagement in the immediate future.

It would be impossible within our space to follow in detail the party history of Belgium for eighty-three years. Its complications are considerable. The kingdom's population in the nineteenth century was quite large enough for its internal affairs to attain an importance, and its statesmen to exhibit a dignity and ability not out of scale with those of the greater European countries. Any one who, like the present writer, has long been familiar with the tone and level of the debates in the Belgian Senate and Chamber will be aware of the great difference between them and the legislatures of many smaller or newer countries. In the latter one may sometimes discover how little the Parliament is removed from the level of a glorified parish council, or Board of Guardians. In Belgium one oftener feels, how well qualified all the principal actors would be to fill the stage at Westminster or the Palais-Bourbon. For the purposes of illustration, therefore, we will content ourselves with tracing briefly the history of what have been perhaps the two leading controversies—that over education, in which the protagonists have been the Catholics and the Liberals, and that over the franchise, which has mainly been fought out between the Catholics and the Socialists.

The Constitution of 1831 made the right of instruction free; *i. e.* anybody who liked could teach or organise a school. The Catholic Church went ahead with a system of primary schools, while the attention of Parliament was at first taken up with Higher Education. After some controversy in 1835–6 the university system was settled on its present basis, viz. two State Universities, at Liége and Ghent respectively, and two "free" Universities, one under Catholic auspices at Louvain, and one under Liberal auspices at Brussels. The number of students attending these universities in modern times is perhaps worth quoting, as showing the distribution of influence. In 1911–12 the figures were: Louvain 2100, Brussels 918, Liége 1803, Ghent 535. In 1842 the last, and not the least notable, of the coalition Ministries, that of M. Nothomb, enacted the first great law on Primary Education. It obtained seventy-five votes to three in the Chamber, and was passed by the Senate unanimously; so that it can be considered to have been at the time a national solution of this thorny problem. The law made it compulsory for every commune to maintain at least one school, where primary education should be given gratuitously. If this school was not sufficient to give all the teaching required, it might either provide more, or "adopt" schools organised by private agencies, *e. g.* the Church; which thereupon received grants from it. The Government and the provincial administrations made grants to the communes towards these objects. The Catholic concession to the Liberals was that a national system of education was set up, under State auspices and subject to Government inspection. The Liberal concession to the Catholics was that the teaching of religion (*i. e.* the Roman Catholic religion) should be obligatory in all such schools, and under the sole control of the clergy, who were entitled to enter the schools at any time to see that it was being properly given. This control covered moral teaching of all kinds, and included a veto over reading-books. The creed taught was to be that of the majority in any school; except in half-a-dozen schools specially organised by Protestants or Jews, this was always Roman Catholic. Although this law lasted thirty-six years, during twenty-two of which the Liberals were in power, it is obvious that it was more favourable to the Catholics than to their opponents. The concession of a State system was inevitable in return for grants of public money; on the other hand the concession of universal control over religion and morals to the Catholic Church, not only in the schools provided by it but in those provided by the communes on behalf of the State, seems only justifiable logically, if the Church were privileged and established under the Constitution, which it expressly was not.

So long as the Liberal party was led by chiefs who had shared the epic experiences of 1831 with the chiefs of the Catholics, the compromise lasted. The first sign of its break-up was in 1868, when the Liberal Ministry, still presided over by Charles Rogier of Liége, perhaps the ablest of the revolutionary heroes, and second to none among the builders of modern Belgium, developed a scheme of schools for adults. Rogier and his colleague Vandenpeereboom, who was in charge of the project, desired to give the clergy admission to these schools on the terms of the law of 1842; but the majority of the Cabinet, composed of younger men, resisted; Rogier was compelled to resign; and with the advent of W. Frère-Orban as Premier the Liberal party entered on a more actively anti-clerical career. Frère-Orban's majority was too weak for him to do much at the time; but when, after an eight years' interval of Catholic rule, he returned to power in 1878, he set promptly and drastically to work. His Education Law of 1879 deprived the clergy of all right of entry into the schools during school hours, and all control over the ordinary school teaching; which was placed on an unde-nominational basis, controlled exclusively by the civil authorities. Religious instruction might still be given in the schools, but only before or after school hours, and rooms were to be put at the disposal of the priests for that purpose. Private (*i. e.* Church) training colleges for teachers were deprived of their authorisation; and the communal councils, in appointing their teaching staff, were compelled to limit their choice to candidates with diplomas from the State schools. The adopted Catholic schools lost their right to grants, and the communes could no longer adopt them. Other steps were taken to diminish the authority of the communes over the schools by the working of a central department of Public Instruction, which was now for the first time set up.

The resistance to this Act by the Catholics bordered on civil war. For many years the number of Catholic schools had diminished, the religious control of the priesthood over the public schools being so thorough that they wished for nothing better. At short notice they saw the whole of this ground cut away under their feet, and resolved to shrink from nothing in order to recover it. On the day the law passed the Senate, a pastoral

letter from the bishops forbade parents, if
they wished for absolution from their sins, to
send their children to the public schools;
and forbade teachers and inspectors to accept
or retain employment in them. The provision of Catholic schools in every parish
was enjoined upon the parish priests; and
throughout the country rich and poor, from
the old Catholic noble families of Arenberg,
Mérode and the rest down to the humblest
peasants, weavers and sempstresses in Flanders, contributed to this end. Barns, stables,
and public-houses were pressed into the
service; new buildings were run up by workmen who declined wages; within twelve
months over 2000 schools of a kind had been
organised by the Catholics on these lines, and
all the children withdrawn from the free
schools had been accommodated. Meanwhile
every pulpit thundered in the cause, preaching
the boycott of Liberal tradesmen and the
eviction of Liberal tenants; while any known
Liberal was refused absolution and the
sacraments, besides every form of temporal
assistance. On the other side some Liberal
employers retaliated by dismissing work-
people unless they sent their children to the
Government schools; and similar pressure
was put on state railwaymen and officials
in government service. The Pope, Leo XIII,

was appealed to by both sides, and affirmed
his desire to mediate; but as all the concessions which he suggested were to come from
the Government, Frère-Orban lost patience
with him and withdrew the Belgian Legation
from the Vatican.

The bitterness of this struggle has probably
never been surpassed in a modern country;
and the social cleavage, which we have
remarked as existing to-day between parties
in Belgium, dates in a large measure from it.
It did infinite harm both to politics and to
education. The State was unable to procure
a teaching staff adequate for its scheme; and
the Catholics were still more unable to man
with qualified teachers their multitude of
mushroom schools. They had to be staffed
somehow; and a great number of unsuitable
persons who thus obtained posts continued
to hold them for long afterwards. The
conflict raged till 1884, with many fluctua-
tions and some genuine though tardy and
unsuccessful attempts by the Ministry to
conciliate their opponents. But at the 1884
elections the Ministry were completely beaten;
the Liberal party went out of office, and it
has never held office since.

The incoming Catholic Ministry was presided over by the veteran Jules Malou, who
besides having been Premier from 1871–1878,

had for many years been the experienced
leader of the Catholic parliamentary Opposition. Malou was a very able man, and not
an extremist; but in such times his party
would have none but extreme measures, and
his subordinates included several strong-
willed men, notably M. Woeste, of an extremely bitter temperament. The Liberal
Education Law, though it had been five years
in force, was summarily repealed and a new
law passed which restored in the main the
principles of 1842. The communes were once
more given wide powers over the education
in their areas; a great number of the communal schools were suppressed as unnecessary;
most of the State Training Colleges were
closed, and the money set free in both cases
went to the corresponding Catholic institutions. The net effect was that, whereas
by 1875 nearly three-quarters of the primary
schools had come to be provided by the
communes and little more than a quarter
by the Church, after the law of 1884 the
proportions were practically reversed. At
the same time religious instruction under the
control of the Church was permitted (though
not made compulsory) in all schools during
school hours and by the regular teachers,
with an exemption clause whereby children
might be excused attendance at it on the

written application of their parents. It was now the turn of the Liberals to make violent protests. While this legislation was passing the Chamber, fierce riots broke out in all the principal cities; and a fortnight before the new law passed the Senate something like a pitched battle between Liberals and Catholics occurred in the streets of Brussels. Shortly afterwards the communal elections took place, at which the Liberals gained such important successes that the King (Leopold II) intervened, and, to mitigate the strife of parties, induced the most unpopular of the Ministers, M. Woeste and another, to resign. Malou resigned with them, and M. Beernaert, a Catholic of much more conciliatory tendencies, became Prime Minister. The new law, however, was not altered.

Down to this point, it will be seen, education in Belgium was free but not compulsory. There had to be schools for the children to attend, but they were not obliged to attend them. This system actually lasted for another thirty years, long after every other European country, except Russia and Turkey, had adopted compulsory education. The results were perhaps not so bad as might have been expected; and no worse than in countries like Spain, where the compulsion is badly enforced. Nevertheless they were bad; and sheer illiteracy remained common in certain districts, especially in Flanders. Moreover, the extensive employment of members of the religious orders as unpaid teachers in the Catholic schools tended to lower the whole standard of payment for teachers, and consequently of efficiency. While the cost of primary education in Belgium was kept abnormally low, its quality remained low also. The true percentage of illiterates among the population has been too much a matter of party controversy to be ascertained without dispute from official returns. When Mr. Rowntree a few years ago conducted, as an English and outside observer, his monumental inquiry into Belgian social conditions, he made an independent investigation into this subject in connection with one into housing; and his results, which covered 13,270 persons of the working class over ten years of age distributed in communes representative of the various types and districts, are probably the fairest obtainable. He found that of the whole 13,270 no less than 21·4 per cent. (18·55 per cent. of the men and 24·50 per cent. of the women) were unable either to read or to write; the percentage between the ages of ten and twenty being 13·43, between twenty and forty 17·98, and over forty no less than 39·13. The figures became still

more striking when analysed geographically.
He found that those from the four great
towns, Brussels, Antwerp, Liége and Ghent
(whose communal administration is always
in Liberal hands), showed an illiterate percentage of 11·75; while, taking those from
the rest of the country, the returns from the
Walloon communes showed a percentage of
17·34, and from the Flemish communes a
percentage of 34·69. The illiterate percentage among people over forty in the Flemish
communes was 58·10. Having regard to the
undisputed fact that these Flemish communes
represent the region of completest Catholic
ascendancy both in education and in everything else, the figures make it difficult to avoid
the conclusion that the Catholic statesmen of
Belgium have seriously sacrificed the interests
of education to those of their party and Church.

After many years of wrangling, in 1895, after
the semi-annihilation of the Liberal party at
the first election held on the widened franchise,
the Catholics carried a further law making
religious instruction compulsory in all schools.
It retained, however, the right of exemption
from religious teaching for children whose
parents expressed the desire for it in writing,
and provided that in schools attended by any
such children, the other teaching should not
be given a definitely Catholic character, but

should be "neutral." This concession came
to be much regretted by Catholics, because in
a good many schools the presence of a few
non-Catholic children made "neutral" instruction inevitable for a much larger number
of Catholic children. Meanwhile the Liberal
attack on the system, now reinforced by the
Socialists, was concentrated on two main
points—the adoption of compulsory education and the abolition of the subsidised
Catholic schools. Whatever be thought of
the second point, which raises the whole
question as to whether private enterprise
and a denominational "religious atmosphere" in education are desirable things,
there can be little doubt that the first point—
compulsory attendance—was essential to reform. Not only were there a considerable
number of children, possibly 10 per cent., who
never attended school at all, but the irregular
attendance of the others made it impossible
for even good teachers to obtain adequate
results. In 1904 a very long and heated
debate on both these points took place in
the Chamber; but the Government, under the
influence of M. Woeste—still, as always,
the prophet of "no compromise" within his
party—refused all concessions. It was not
till 1912 that a comprehensive Bill was introduced by the then Premier, M. Schollaert;

but this came to nothing, and M. Schollaert resigned. His successor, Baron de Broqueville, was more fortunate, and the Bill which his Ministry introduced in 1913 passed into law the following year. Under this measure attendance at school has been for the first time made compulsory, and the teachers in all primary schools, whether provided by the communes or the Church, are to be subject to a government examination, and paid on a uniform scale by the State. Moreover, the " neutrality " which was enjoined by the law of 1895 is no longer to imply abstention from teaching what Catholics call " Christian morality," but only from attacks against the personalities or religious convictions of families whose children attend the schools.

This law was passed such a short time before the outbreak of the European War that it is impossible to say how far in its working it may heal the old conflict and enable the line of party division to be drawn in Belgium over some other issue than that of education. It would be good for Belgium if it could; and it should be noticed that in the higher branches of education, where the blighting influence of this controversy has not been felt in the same degree, the needs of the nation have long been much more adequately met.

Let us now turn to the other great party controversy, that over the franchise. Agitation against the old system dates from the period (1878–1884) of the last Liberal Ministry, which was gravely divided over it. Frère-Orban staved off a party split by giving the vote in provincial and communal elections to *capacitaires*, that is, roughly speaking, to those who now get an extra vote on the score not of property, but of education. But at the end of 1884, when the fire of the great educational struggle had for the time burnt itself out, the franchise issue was revived; and the Liberal party in Brussels split into two hostile groups, the *Doctrinaires*, who did not want manhood suffrage, and the *Progressistes*, who did. In the following year (1885) the present Labour party was established with a socialistic programme, and its propaganda was stimulated by an economic crisis. In 1886, the Walloon provinces became the scene of strikes, which were almost insurrections. They began in the district between Liége and Namur; factories were burned; convents and country-houses were pillaged; there were bloody interventions by the military, and numbers were killed and wounded in the restoration of order. Before it was restored, the revolt had spread westward to Charleroi and Mons; and the sky was

reddened nightly by the glare of terrible
conflagrations. This portentous upheaval of
the industrial masses had behind it little
leadership or plan. It was a blind rising of
famished workmen against miserable wages
and degraded conditions which had stood
still amid the vast progress of their industry.
Men of all parties were impressed; and M.
Beernaert's Government carried a good deal
of remedial legislation, some of which, e. g.
the Housing Law of 1889, has since proved
of considerable value.

This movement of revolt, together with the
almost simultaneous and rapid success achieved
by Socialist co-operative stores in Brussels,
Ghent, and elsewhere, put the Socialist party
on its feet. Hitherto it had been but a
handful of enthusiasts grouped round César
de Paepe; now it became a popular force.
In 1889 the Government prosecuted twenty
Socialists at Mons; they were nearly all
acquitted, and the credit from the trials
mostly went to the accused. At the end
of that year there was a great strike at
Charleroi; in the following year there was one
at Mons. In 1891, on May 2 a great political
strike on behalf of the franchise broke out
among the colliers of Mons, Charleroi and
Liége, which lasted till July 9, and was
swollen after the first week by the adhesion

of the metalworkers. To these strike tactics,
the ultimate surrender of the class which
monopolised the narrow franchise was due.
In 1892 the Chambers passed the formal
resolutions to amend the Constitution, and
were dissolved in June. The elections gave
a majority of the Catholics, but not a two-
thirds majority, so that they could not carry
revision without some support from the
Liberals. The crucial debate began in November, to the accompaniment of riots at
Brussels and Ghent. It was long and violent;
many alternatives were discussed; at last,
on April 12, 1893, all the revisionist proposals
were rejected by the Chamber. Thereupon
the popular storm broke again. The Walloon
miners struck. At Mons the civic guard had
to fire, and killed four; and in the capital
itself there was a furious riot. The very
pillars of society shook, and under unexampled
pressure the Conservatives gave way. On
April 18 the compromise described in Chapter
VII, conceding manhood suffrage, but qualify-
ing it by a plural vote, was adopted by the
Chamber; the assent of the Senate followed on
April 27, and the strikes ended. In 1894 the
first elections took place under the new system;
the Catholics obtained 104 seats, the Liberals
only 19; while the Socialists, who had
previously had no representation, secured 29.

The new system had proved favourable to the Catholics beyond anticipation; and it did not long content the Socialists. If the reader turns to the table of votes and voters given in the last chapter, he can easily understand why. By 1899 the Socialists and Radicals, not supported by the moderate Liberals, brought the matter once more to a crisis; and having before found violence so efficacious, they naturally resorted to it again. This time they were much less successful. The advanced Liberals acted with them to a certain point, and the Chamber had to concede further reform; but the reform obtained was that in which the Liberals were mainly interested, viz. Proportional Representation, and not what the Socialists most desired, viz. the abolition of the plural votes. We have described the system of Proportional Representation in the last chapter, and we need only add that its immediate political effect was to restore to the Liberal party a considerable representation in the Chamber, while checking, on the whole, the growth of the Socialists. Consequently in 1902 the Socialists attempted yet a third political strike with the same object as the last. It was an imposing movement, but a complete political failure; nothing whatever was gained, and the Socialist party which had played the card of violence too often for the taste of the average Belgian, lost a good deal of prestige.

In the following ten years the Catholics maintained their majority, and successive elections convinced all their opponents that, while the plural vote lasted, they would long continue to do so. Accordingly at the " partial " election of 1912, the united Liberal party under M. Paul Hymans made a *cartel*, or election alliance, with the Socialists on the platform of " universal suffrage," *i. e.* the abolition of the plural votes. But the alliance frightened moderate Liberal electors into voting for the Catholics, and the latter actually increased their majority. Popular disappointment in the great towns was acute, and on June 30 a special Conference of the Socialist party decided to organise a general strike. Preparations were to be made for it throughout the winter, and it was to begin on April 14, 1913. The strike was carried out, and unlike those of 1891–1893 and their successors in 1899 and 1902, it was free from violence or bloodshed. But again it was politically a failure. After a short time, the best which the Socialist leaders could hope was to obtain some nominal concession which might enable the strike to be abandoned, and it also became the Government's interest to make such a concession in order to end the incident

without bloodshed. The difficulty was to
bring the two parties together on this basis
without appearing to humble one or other
of them; but after two mediations by the
Burgomasters of the four great cities, the
strike was ended on the Prime Minister's
consenting to appoint a Commission to report
on the system of voting for provincial and
communal elections, with the proviso that if
the Commission made any suggestion appli-
cable to the elections for the Chambers, the
Government would allow it to be discussed.

Beyond this point the matter has not yet
progressed; but with the dying off of the
older generation among Catholic politicians,
it would not be surprising if the party
abolished, or at least diminished, the plural
votes of its own accord. Its advanced
sections, which are ably represented in the
Ministry, have long urged this course; and
though it would increase the Socialist representation in the Chambers, it seems probable
that the Liberals rather than the Catholics
would be weakened by it, as was the case with
the original extension of the franchise in 1894.
It would be a gain for the Catholic party for its
power to be seen resting on the democracy
instead of appearing to rest on the plural voter.
A party which claims, and possibly with justice,
to represent the majority, endangers that claim

by perpetuating the rule of the minority as if it were vital to its existence.

In both the controversies which we have traced, the reader will remark, and may deplore, the tendency to coerce Parliament by extra-parliamentary violence. The revolutionary example was first set by the Catholic party, *i. e.* the party of the Conservatives and the old nobility, in the years 1879–1884. It was copied by their opponents, the Liberal middle class, when the Catholics won the upper hand; and when the downtrodden proletariat started shaking society in 1886, it was merely acting on a lesson which had been recently and plentifully taught to it by its social superiors. The Belgian Catholics were not the first Conservative party in history, and may not be the last, to find, when too late for repentance, that if one starts constitutional and social incendiarism the flames cannot be confined to other people's houses. The Socialists who invoked violence to destroy the old monopolist franchise had at least this excuse, peculiar to franchise agitations, that a parliamentary remedy was not really open to them, since Parliament was elected by the very body whose monopoly they attacked. This inherent element of justice in the agitation of 1891–1893 had much to do with its triumph. The subsequent attempts to repeat it, and their failure, followed what seems to be a definite psychological tendency in modern democracies. Political success attained by violence infects those who have attained it with a belief that they can get more by the same methods, and it simultaneously infects the large peace-loving public with a growing determination that they shall not. There can be very little doubt that, while the recurrent strike agitations have nourished the zeal of the Socialist party's zealots, they have prevented it more than anything else from widening its electoral influence as far as the great ability of its parliamentary leaders entitled it to expect. In point of fact its representation in the Chamber to-day, is no larger a fraction of that body (whose membership has been increased in conformity with the growth of the population) than it was when it entered Parliament twenty years ago.

The excesses of the later strife between Belgian parties scarcely correspond to the normal temper of the Belgian people, which is stable and law-abiding. Nor should they blind us to the marked success, on the whole, of Belgian parliamentary institutions. No-where on the Continent has the machinery of parliamentary and Cabinet Government imported from England worked so consistently

G

well for so long a time; and only perhaps in
Holland and the Scandinavian countries is
it now on an equally stable footing. There is
not in Belgium, as there is in France, any
large body of opinion desiring a fundamental
change in the relations between Parliament
and the Executive. The Socialists advocate
a Republic, *i. e.* the substitution of election
for heredity in the choice of the titular head
of the State; but while the change is one on
whose democratic utility the world's experience
seems to throw increasing doubt, it is certainly
not one whose advocacy swells the votes of
the Socialist party. The three monarchs who
have in succession occupied the throne of
Belgium have all wielded a great influence
over its affairs; but in each case this has been
far more due to a strong personality than to
any formal prerogatives which have been
conferred by the Constitution, or could be
withdrawn by amending it.

TABLE SHOWING THE CONSTITUTION OF PARTIES IN THE
CHAMBER AFTER THE LAST FIVE (PARTIAL) ELECTIONS.

	1906.	1908.	1910.	1912.	1914.
Catholics	89	87	88	101	99
Liberals	46	43	45	45	45
Socialists	30	35	34	38	40
Christian Democrats	1	1	1	2	2

CHAPTER IX

SOCIAL CONDITIONS AND AGENCIES

BELGIUM is the land with the densest population in Europe; the cheapest railway travelling and railway rates; and the smallest average size of land-holdings. The population is much spread out; nowhere else do so many urban workers have their homes in the country. It is a hive of mining and manufacturing industries; and at the same time its agricultural production in proportion to area is the highest in the world. Wages are very low; and trade unionism is weak. On the other hand, costs of living, and especially of housing, are also low; and co-operative movements of several kinds are strong. The birthrate is practically the same as the British; the deathrates in the great towns are lower. There is a good judicial system; a fairly efficient police; and an extremely inefficient Poor Law. There is a great amount of philanthropic effort, but its motive is practically always political or (what is almost the same thing in Belgium) religious; and while the competition of parties gives it a powerful stimulus, it also leads to much overlapping and dissipation of effort.

The most formative of modern influences in Belgium has been the railway system; by which the later developments of its industry, agriculture and housing have been incalculably assisted. Thanks to the business acumen of Leopold I, Belgium possessed the first railways on the Continent. The King, who was closely in touch with English engineers and industrialists, shared George Stephenson's view, which the British House of Commons rejected, in favour of a State system. The centre of this was originally at Malines, with four lines radiating thence to the principal great towns; that through Brussels being extended to Charleroi, and thence linked up with France. Later, under the mid-century Liberal Governments, concessions were given to various private companies; but these have been since absorbed; and practically the whole of the full-gauge railways are now in the State system. The figures on December 31, 1911, were—State lines 2697 miles; private: 218 miles. The light railways amounted at that date to another 2420 miles; while 464 miles of light railways were under construction. Of this system it may be said broadly, in contradistinction to the British, that no part of its capital represents watered stock, or the cost of constructing rival lines in competition between identical places, or the cost of renewals wrongly carried to capital account by a generation hungry for dividends; still less such expenditure as that in England over Parliamentary Bills. The traveller or the consigner of goods on the Belgian railways has to pay, of course, for the cost of their construction and management; but he has not to pay also for a past accumulation of mistakes and jobberies, nor to pile up profits for private shareholders.

Since 1885 the main railway system has been supplemented by a very complete system of light railways. These are practically steam tramways, running most commonly on the high-roads. They each belong to a separate limited company; but are all constructed and controlled by a central company, the " National Society for Local Railways " (*Société Nationale de Chemins-de-fers Vicinaux*), which is administered by a council of four, two appointed by the Crown, and two by the shareholders in the different lines voting as one body. The chairman of the council is appointed by the Crown, as is the general manager; while there is a supervising committee of nine elected members, one from the shareholders of each province. The provision of the railways is effected between this company, the State, the provinces, and the communes on a very ingenious plan. First there is an application from the commune (or communes) to the National Society, which makes a rough survey and estimates, and submits them to the Government. If the Government approves, a limited company is formed to make the line. The State, in return for a right of final control over the plans, subscribes half the capital, and the province subscribes a third or a quarter. The rest is mainly found by the communes, and a very small fraction by private individuals. The State, the provinces, and the communes do not provide their capital in a lump, but pay it in annual instalments for ninety years to the National Society. These instalments have been fixed at $3\frac{1}{2}$ per cent. or a little more on the capital subscribed; and as there is the State guarantee of the principal, the National Society has been able to issue 3 per cent. debentures. The lines are thus cheaply financed, and if a company's line can earn a higher percentage than the annual instalments, there is, after payment to certain reserve funds, an actual return of profit to the public bodies investing in it. The National Society provides rolling stock, but farms out the working of the lines to companies, in which the communes, again, are not infrequently the principal shareholders. This system deserves some attention from those interested in " hybrid " schemes to combine public and private enterprise. Its merits are, that capital has been cheaply provided without an excessive burden on the public; that the State has kept full control over construction; that the National Society has formed a central reservoir of skilled advice and experience; and that at the same time each line has had a close and personal management, and each locality a direct interest in making its line prosper.

The great system of internal waterways is also almost entirely under public control. It is not worked to make profits, but to serve trade. Together with the cheap fares and freights of the main State railways, it has been used to decentralise Belgian industry into the small or moderate-sized industrial centres, which are such a marked feature of it. An extraordinarily cheap system of weekly tickets for workmen enables employees to

live at great distances from their work. Not
a few travel every day from distances of
sixty miles or more; and distances up to
thirty miles are almost a matter of indifference. The result is that both manufacturer
and workman bear perhaps a lighter burden
of rent in Belgium than in any other country;
and the problems of housing and hygiene are
incalculably eased. The long hours in Belgian
factories render the hours of travel an oppressive and exhausting addition for many toilers;
but the possession of a country home, usually
with a little land, has many advantages,
especially for the children, and proves particularly helpful in times of unemployment.
In many seasonal trades, such as the building
industry, there are very large numbers of
workmen, who combine (or rather alternate)
town work with work on the land; and thus
get rid of the problem of unemployment in
a very practical way. The ubiquitous light
railways supplement these processes; but
their greatest benefits are for agriculture.
Acting as feeders to and from the main lines,
they convey enormous quantities of produce,
cattle, manures, fertilisers and fodder through
the rural districts, besides coal, timber, stone,
gravel, sand, lime, bricks, etc.; and they have
not only enriched the cultivated areas, but

brought others into cultivation in the Campine and the Ardennes.

The land in Belgium is divided between an unusually large number of owners. The true figure cannot be ascertained from the official returns, which show separate properties, not proprietors; but Mr. Rowntree's inquiry, a few years ago, showed that 10 per cent. of the population owned at least a plot, and 47 per cent. of the soil was owned by persons with not more than a hundred acres. This extreme subdivision seems mainly due to the operation during the nineteenth century of the Belgian laws of testamentary and intestate succession. These laws forbid property to be entailed, and with certain exceptions they compel it to be equally divided among the legal heirs. With the prevalent small ownership there goes a prevalence of small agricultural holdings. Leaving out of account those under one acre, Mr. Rowntree found the average size of farms in Belgium to be fourteen and a half acres, as compared with sixty-three in Great Britain. Of the agricultural population 65 per cent. are farmers and the members of their families working with them; only 35 per cent. are labourers. In Great Britain the percentages are reversed, and 70 per cent. are labourers.

But it must not be supposed from this

G 2

that the small cultivators and small proprietors are always the same people. In the most intensively farmed areas, those of Flanders, the peasants are usually tenants at a rack rent on comparatively short leases. Owing to the great subdivision of the land, its rents and prices rule very high, because there are more competitors for small lettings than for large. Indeed, the peasants can only pay them by putting up with a standard of life far lower than their productivity warrants; nor could they even so, if it were not for the great advance in technical methods, the use of artificial manures, etc., which a very good system of agricultural education has enabled them to make. They have also, as we shall see, been assisted by the development of agricultural co-operation, and co-operative banks mainly through Catholic agencies. But the unsatisfactory feature of Belgian rural life, at least so far as Flanders is concerned, is that all these improvements sooner or later, and mostly sooner, are balanced by rises in rent; and though the wealth of the country grows, that of the cultivators does not. In the more sparsely populated parts of Belgium, such as the Ardennes and Limburg, the cultivators are really more prosperous. To a greater extent they own what they cultivate; and they are materially helped by rights of common, which in those areas have not been wholly extinguished.

The presence of this teeming agricultural population on the soil of Flanders and Brabant, accustomed to hard work and cheap living, and often seeking only subsidiary and intermittent employment in the town, has helped to keep down Belgian industrial wages. The low scale of these may be also explained by the weakness of trade unionism, a feature which in itself seems to have four separate causes. These are :

(1) The dispersal of the workers' homes over large areas, and the time daily consumed by them in travelling. English trade unionists know, how, even in London, the distance between homes and work-places weakens their organisations, whenever there is not, as there is at Woolwich, or by the Docks, a strong nucleus of resident labour. This difficulty affects nearly all Belgian unions in an unusual degree.

(2) The strength of local and provincial sentiment, which led to the growth of little unions in each separate centre.

(3) The great prevalence of home work, and also of small workshops.

(4) The fact that trade unions, like nearly all other Belgian organisations, have been political in origin, and that the cleavage between the parties is too wide for unions under different party flags to co-operate, much less to unite. At present there are Socialist unions, Catholic unions and Liberal unions; and though the first are much the strongest, they have by no means a monopoly. Now in an enterprise like co-operation such a division of forces does no vital harm. A Socialist co-operative store with 2000 members can flourish exceedingly, even though a Catholic co-operative store with 1000 members and a Liberal co-operative store with 500 stand in the same street. But the success or failure of a trade union depends on its including as far as possible *all* the workers in a given trade; and if the trade membership is divided out in any such proportions as the foregoing no one of the three unions can exert much strength in collective bargaining. This is perhaps the fundamental reason why the Belgian Labour movement, political in its inception and still predominantly political in its inspiration, while able to make a success of the co-operative store, has by comparison failed with the trade union. It may be rejoined, that a similar political origin has

not prevented the German Socialist trade
unions from becoming a great force in their
own field. But there are few if any parts of
Germany where the political schism within
the working-class itself is so deep-rooted,
as that which prevents a Belgian Catholic
workman from joining a trade union under
Socialist auspices.

Some of these weaknesses in Belgian trade
unionism are being in a measure overcome.
The Socialists have worked hard at fusing
local trade unions, and also at creating a
federal organisation between the unions in
different trades. The Trade Union Committee
(*Commission Syndicale*), which the Labour
Party has formed and to which various
" independent " trade unions are affiliated,
holds annual trade union congresses; and
although housed at the Socialist headquarters
in Brussels, contains the germs of a dis-
tinctively trade union statesmanship. The
delegates at its last congress (1914) represented
126,745 members. Its leaders seek their
models mainly in the German federation of
trade unions. French Syndicalist ideas have
not greatly affected them, and are scarcely
adapted for the Flemish temperament, though
they may be for the Walloon; but there is a
desire among some of the trade union chiefs

to make their organisations less political. The
Belgian Labour movement started with the
idea, to which that of Great Britain has
slowly, partially, and recently attained, that
all the efforts of the working-class to uplift
itself, whether by political, trade unionist,
or co-operative action, ought to be linked
together in one organisation, as so many concerted moves by the single working-class army.
Undoubtedly the politicians have benefited
most by this arrangement, and the trade
unions least. Yet there have been some
benefits to all the parties, particularly on the
educational side.

The Belgian co-operative movement, so far
as regards consumers' societies, is on a small
scale in comparison with the British; and
with negligible exceptions is under party
auspices. After several non-party co-operative failures, the Socialists were first successful
with the famous society " Vooruit " at Ghent
(1881), followed by the " Maison du Peuple "
at Brussels (1882). These societies were
started by poor men with very small resources
(the wage rates at Ghent are the lowest in the
Belgian great towns) in a high spirit of
political and educational idealism. Both have
long been extremely flourishing; and prosperity has not quenched that early spirit so

noticeably as in the case of many English co-operative concerns. The Socialists were not long in transplanting co-operation to the Walloon county, where they are politically strongest; and the greater number of their stores are now situated there. The movement has a "Wholesale," the *Fédération des Sociétés coopératives Belges*, whose sales have risen from £30,694 in 1901 to £382,654 in 1912—still rather modest figures, if judged by English or Scottish standards. The Federation includes a certain number of co-operative producing societies, which the larger consuming societies have floated as subsidiary enterprises. The "Vooruit," for instance, has organised a co-operative and spinning society at Ghent; and in the same town under the same auspices there is a co-operative printing society and a co-operative society of builders. The "Vooruit's" total receipts in 1912 were about £164,105, and its membership was about 8000—a figure which had not altered substantially for a number of years. The "Maison du Peuple" at Brussels in 1912 had a membership of 20,000, but its sales were only £271,795. The next largest society, "Le Progrès" of Jolimont, with a membership also about 20,000, and branches in many coal and iron townships throughout the

Centre coalfield, had sales of £184,000. It will be seen that the value of the purchases per head is extremely low. In Ghent it is about half the English average per head; in the Centre coalfield it is less than a quarter. Even when allowance is made for the much lower wages and smaller weekly expenditure of the Belgian workman, it is clear that any direct service rendered by co-operation as a factor in his housekeeping, must be far less in Belgium. The same conclusion would be reached if we examined figures for the Catholic and Liberal co-operative societies. The Liberals have only one society, that at Antwerp, which may be called flourishing; and the Catholics, whose largest society is at Charleroi, have nowhere succeeded in overtaking the start which the Socialists obtained in this work.

But it would be wrong to measure the performance of the Belgian co-operative stores solely by English standards. Their aims have been different. They have not sought primarily to add sixpence or a shilling per week to the value of the workman's earnings, their object has rather been to enable people earning very low wages to obtain those benefits of political organisation, trade-unionism, and education, for which they were too poor to

pay solely by direct contributions. Co-operation, it is often said in Belgium, carries
Socialism and trade-unionism on its back.
The profits on sales have built fine premises,
which all three movements use; they also
enable direct grants to be made to politics
and propaganda, and have helped to finance
not a few strikes. But the help has not all
been on one side. It was a loan of £80 from
a trade union, the Ghent Weavers' Association, which enabled the " Vooruit " to be
founded; and the history of non-political co-
operation in Belgium, both in the eight years
before that, when it had the field to itself
(the first non-political society started in 1873),
and in the thirty-three years since, gives
ground for doubting whether the movement
could have been seriously developed without
a political or religious stimulus. On its present lines it has had a great educational
influence; local increases of thrift and de-
creases in gin-drinking seem often traceable
to it. Scientific, literary, musical and gym-
nastic societies all flourish among the workmen under the co-operative roof; and the
Socialist, who looks forward to a future of
democratic culture attained by fraternal effort
and the spontaneity of the working-class, has
many justifications for finding in the social

and corporate life of a great society, like the
" Maison du Peuple " or the " Vooruit," the
best foretaste of his ideal.

The Catholic party's co-operative stores
require no special notice. Its real equivalent to the Socialist enterprises must be
sought in the country side. Space does not
allow us to give any minute description of
Belgian agriculture, which was investigated
in special detail not long ago by Mr. Rowntree. We have said it is typically, though
not solely, an agriculture of small holdings;
and its production per acre is the highest
in Europe. Comparing Belgium with Great
Britain, France, Germany, Holland, and Denmark, we find that she keeps per square mile
more cattle and more pigs than any of them
except Holland, and more horses than any
but Holland and Denmark; that her yields
of wheat and oats per acre are the highest
of all, and she is also at the top with sugar
beet and potatoes. She has less permanent
grass-land than any of the others; and
though her capacity to feed her population
has fallen steadily with the growth of her
towns and industries, she still feeds more
persons per square mile than any of her
neighbours. Her consumption per head of
fruit and vegetables is higher than that in

Great Britain, and yet her exports of both exceed her imports. These results have been obtained without any tariff protection, save for oats, meat, and butter, although the soil is not naturally rich, and in the area of the Great Plain is decidedly poor. For all this there appear to be four main explanations—

(1) The people's traditional aptitude for agriculture which originated in the eighteenth century;

(2) The great subdivision of holdings which occurred mainly in the nineteenth;

(3) The development of agricultural education;

(4) The development of co-operative agencies among the farmers.

The credit for both the last two really belongs to the modern Catholic Party; and one might cite as a practical illustration of their effect, the fact that Belgium uses a greater weight of chemical manures per square mile than any other country in the world.

Agricultural education is organised by the State; it includes both the special training given in agricultural colleges and more popular instruction, which is made widely available for working cultivators. For the latter purpose the country is mapped out into districts, to each of which a State expert (*agronome*) is attached. These agronomes have charge of State experimental plots; they also organise a large number of lectures to farmers and farmers' wives; and their habit is to attend local markets and meetings to keep in personal touch with the cultivators and to give them as much free advice as they care to ask for. The system has become exceedingly effective, because it has been put on this thoroughly local and personal footing. Although in too many parts of the country its final result has been to raise rents rather than to enrich the cultivators, it has greatly increased the productivity of farming, and made it possible to farm land which before was not worth reclaiming.

Although as we have said this education has been mainly the work of Catholic statesmen, it is in the Walloon rather than the Flemish provinces that it has been most keenly utilised. The State has also created organisations of farmers; but for most purposes beside the holding of agricultural shows, they have been superseded by private organisations. The latter are again the work of Catholics; and from the famous *Boerenbond* downwards, are closely connected with the Church's parochial machinery. As a rule there is a separate society in every village and these are gathered into large district federations. They are formed for a great number of purposes—to insure live-stock or houses, to improve the breeds of animals, to provide cultivators with capital, to effect the co-operative purchase of seeds and manures, and to effect the co-operative handling and sale of dairy and other products. The village scale on which most of these societies are worked enables their expenses to be kept extremely low; and for a great many of them the parish priest, in a secretarial capacity, acts as an unpaid and very hard-working factotum. The federal organisation keeps them on sound lines, and enables them to consolidate their operations, whenever there is an economic advantage in conducting these on a larger scale. The interactions of this great movement with that of agricultural education can be easily understood. For instance, if it is a question of artificial manures, a co-operative purchasing society can not only buy them much more cheaply for the cultivator than he could buy them for himself, but can guarantee their quality. The introduction of the Raiffeisen banking system from Germany in 1892 gave a special and far-reaching stimulus; and in hundreds of villages

co-operative credit institutions of this type are
now firmly established. These are only used by
the smaller cultivators. For the larger farmers
there are a number of larger agricultural
banks (*comptoirs agricoles*) under Government
auspices, which do a considerable business.

The co-operative agricultural movement,
which we have described, does not differ in
its general features from those which have
been set on foot among the peasants of Denmark, Holland, Germany, and latterly of
Ireland. But its scale and success, and the
elasticity with which it has been applied to
the peculiar needs of the country are worthy
of admiration. The religio-political philanthropy, of which it is the outcome, rather
than of any spontaneous action by the
peasants, takes a great many forms in Belgium.
The least satisfactory may be seen in connection with the Poor Law. The local Poor Law
areas are the 2632 communes, whose individual resources for this purpose can be
augmented by pious donors. Where, as not
seldom happens, the funds thus to be administered are considerable, a demoralisation
is apt to follow, recalling but surpassing what
may be sometimes noticed in charity-ridden
English Cathedral towns. The scale of relief
comes to be varied according to the religion

and politics of the recipient, and there has
even been a not infrequent tendency to pay
grants in relief of low wages.

Belgian philanthropy, though not the monopoly of the Catholic party, has its roots in
the practice of the Catholic Church, and has
not always purged away its mediæval features.
But it often works, and has sometimes been
a pioneer, in admirable and ultra-modern
directions. We might quote two examples
from a single locality. One is the famous
" Ghent system " of insurance against unemployment (since copied in England and
elsewhere), whereby public grants were made
to trade unions in proportion to their expenditure on unemployment benefit. The
other is the institution of " schools for
mothers," which during the last ten years
has been so successfully used to reduce in-
fantile mortality in most civilised countries.
This idea originated with Dr. Van Miele of
Ghent, who started the first " school for
mothers " in 1901 in that city.

It remains for us briefly to notice the social
policy of the Belgian State. Till 1886 it
scarcely existed; and it is still backward.
The Liberals disliked State interference any-
where; the Catholics were suspicious of its
intrusion upon what they considered to be

the province of religion and charity. So far as concerns the fostering of industry and agriculture, the national line has been tolerably clear. Belgium puts little trust in protective tariffs, but much in State-provided facilities for transport. She has almost the lowest tariff on the Continent; wheat and many necessaries come in free; and the average customs duty on the dutiable articles is less than 1·5 per cent. On the other hand, her State-controlled railway and canal system have been, as we have shown, the mainspring of her modern development. What, then, of factory legislation, of mines regulation, of sanitary and housing legislation—in a word, of all the machinery of State interference by which modern countries seek to safeguard the wage-earner and his family from the worst of the oppressions, against which they are individually powerless? What has been done by the State, in this land of low wages and high illiteracy, to avert the grinding of the faces of the poor?

There have been two chief periods of social legislation. The first was after the revolutionary upheaval of the Walloon workers in 1886. M. Beernaert, who was then the Catholic Prime Minister, represented the progressive wing of his party. A statesman of

much culture, an eminent international lawyer, and a Catholic deeply penetrated with
the spirit of which Leo XIII's encyclical
Rerum Novarum is the best-known expression,
he succeeded in carrying a series of humani-
tarian laws in the face of strong opposition
both from the *laisser-faire* Liberals and from
the more Conservative elements on his own
side of the Chamber. The Liberal attitude
in these matters had perhaps not a little to
do with the sensational repudiation of Liberalism by the enlarged electorate in 1894. M.
Beernaert's work comprised a law prohibiting
the truck system (1887); a factory law excluding children under twelve from factories
and fixing hours of labour for male workers
under sixteen and females under twenty-one
(1889); an important Housing Law (1889);
and a law on Friendly Societies (1894). These
laws, excepting the last but one, were not
intrinsically remarkable; for instance, the
restriction of factory hours left them exceedingly long. Yet a start had been made.
Unfortunately M. Beernaert ceased to be
Prime Minister in 1894 owing to a dispute
with his party over Proportional Representation; and during the following ten years his
influence with successive governments was
eclipsed by the reactionary influence of

M. Woeste. Legislation was initiated in various new directions, but always kept within the narrowest limits. For instance, in 1900 a law was passed comprising an old-age pension on workmen over sixty-five who were in need; but the amount paid was fixed at 1s. per week. An official inquiry in 1895 showed that 35 per cent. of the industrial workers were employed seven days per week; but it was not till 1905 that a law enjoined a six-day limit save where special exemptions were granted (as they since have too freely been). Meanwhile, there grew up within the Catholic party a young and able group of Parliamentarians, who inherited M. Beernaert's spirit and wished to carry social legislation much further than he had been able to do. After years of bickering with the dominant Conservative school represented by such men as MM. Woeste and Delbeke, this party of the " Young Right " brought things to a crisis in 1907, when, with the veteran M. Beernaert's co-operation, it inflicted a severe defeat on the Government over the question of limiting the hours of miners. The shock of this victory was considerable. It was accentuated by a victory of the same party in the following year on another class issue—the question whether conscripts drawn for military service should be allowed, if rich enough, to purchase exemption. The rebels obtained a footing in the Cabinet, which has been steadily increased; and in the 1911–1914 Ministry of Baron de Broqueville their influence was definitely in the ascendant. So began a second era of social legislation, cut short by the outbreak of war. We mentioned in the last chapter the enactment of compulsory education by this Cabinet. Almost contemporaneously it carried a great measure of National Insurance against sickness, invalidity, and old age. This law is mainly modelled after German and English legislation. It has been grafted on a Pensions Law of March 1911 and on a long series of measures whereby the State had subsidised thrift societies; and it adopts the principle of obligatory contributions to be paid in certain proportions by the insured and the employer and supplemented by the State. The many existing insurance and benefit societies are brought into the machinery of the scheme. Down to the outbreak of the European War its prospects of working were satisfactory; but it was too recent for an opinion to be formed of its ultimate success. It is an interesting example of the trend in such matters; but its terms are not sufficiently

generous for a country like Great Britain to
learn much from it.

The only one of M. Beernaert's laws whose
working has shown better results than those
obtained in other countries is the Housing
Law of 1889. Its object was twofold—to
stimulate warfare against slumdom, and to
enable workmen to get new houses built for
them. For the first, it did not need to confer
new powers on the local authorities; for the
Burgomasters have from early times had most
drastic powers (if they care to use them) over
unsatisfactory buildings. What it did was
to set up local committees, nominated partly
by the Central Government and partly by the
Provincial Councils, with the duty of im-
proving housing conditions. At the same
time it carried out its second object so in-
geniously that workmen have been able at
low interest to borrow up to nine-tenths of
the money requisite to buy a site and build
a cottage on it. The machinery was rather
like that adopted for building light railways.
The money is lent by the National Savings
Bank (empowered by the Housing Law to
lend for this purpose up to a fixed limit);
and it is lent to local Credit Associations.
These are companies formed of philanthropic
and substantial people, who subscribe a

nominal capital and pay up one-tenth of it, their liability for the other nine-tenths being the bank's security. Interest on their shares is limited to 3 per cent. The workman who desires a house borrows from the Credit Association at a rate of interest only a fraction above what the bank charges. He also repays the principal by instalments (within twenty-five years), and pays an additional 1 per cent. to insure his life. His total payments on the borrowed capital are about $7\frac{1}{2}$ per cent. till redemption, when he becomes the owner of his house.

In the years 1890–1905 no less than 141,439 houses were built for workmen purchasers in this way. By 1910 there were 208 Credit Associations at work, and about 110,000 workmen had been enabled to become owners of their houses. The low cost of building in Belgium and the marvellous facilities for locomotion have both co-operated towards these results. In 1914 the analogy with the light railway legislation was increased by a law instituting a National Society of Cheap Dwellings to serve as the crown of the system. Housing is, on the whole perhaps, the brightest spot in the Belgian worker's outlook; it is certainly the one where State intervention has been most wisely directed.

CHAPTER X

ART AND LITERATURE

WHEN Pausanias in the reign of Hadrian roamed amid the dead past of Greece, he observed that for every good Greek poem you could find a multitude of good sculptures—the latter indeed were everywhere. Substitute paintings for sculptures, and the remark is true of Belgium. In their great historic epochs the genius of the people was not turned to literature. It is true that some of the better known French writers of those periods—Philippe de Comines, for instance, and Froissart—came from the Low Countries; and later the war against Philip II produced one great writer, Marnix de St. Aldegonde. But these are little in the balance as against the great mass of painting in Flanders and Brabant during the fifteenth, sixteenth, and seventeenth centuries. In the modern period, since the Revolution of 1830, the disparity is less marked. Belgian literature, both in the French language and the Flemish, has some very great names; and these are not isolated phenomena, but the outstanding figures of considerable schools. Since the Revolution more than 100,000 distinct works have been published in Belgium, and a number relatively even greater of reviews and periodicals. Nevertheless it remains true that painting is the people's characteristic art; and taking the modern period alone, where you find tens or scores of remarkable books, you find many hundreds of remarkable pictures. Of the latter, it is hardly too much to repeat Pausanias' phrase that " they are everywhere."

The decay of Belgian town life in the eighteenth century was accompanied by the almost total eclipse of Flemish painting. The traditions of Rubens, Jordaens, Van Dyck, and Teniers had no one to carry them on, and a few graceful colourists, like Lens, alone lightened the darkness. With the rule of Napoleon over Belgium, its art became dominated by the alien classicism of David; and towards 1830 the painters of this school represented at least a numerical revival. None of them are now worth recalling, save perhaps the portrait painter, F. J. Navez. But with the political revolution came something like a resurrection of Belgian art, and it has shown remarkable vigour ever since.

The late Camille Lemonnier once grouped its developments under four periods, or four successive impulses; and if the reader is careful to remember that all these periods to some extent overlap, and the birth of one impulse can be traced much earlier than the exhaustion of another, he may find the classification helpful.

The first period extends roughly from 1830–1850; its art is romantic, heroic, dramatic and patrician; its productions were historical pictures. The second impulse was at its height between 1850 and 1870; it is bourgeois and realistic; its output was genre painting. The third period, some of whose exponents are still alive, was a period of art for art's sake, with a return to the spirit, though not the technique, of the age of Rubens. Its work is full of red blood, pagan, sensuous, exultant, lavish in its manifestations of life. Its subjects and technique were exceedingly varied; but it found its most typical expression in landscape, the expression of a Nature-worshipping pantheism. The fourth period has continued and developed the third in the direction of a subtler perception of light and the influences of light upon forms; with more consciousness, too, of the mystery of life behind its external manifestations.

All these schools show the influence of Paris. The first coincides with the French romantic movement, of Delacroix and Delaroche in painting, and Hugo's *Hernani* in literature. The second is in touch with the genre painting of the Second Empire, which had its literary counterpart in the drama of Dumas *fils*. The third owed much at the outset to such influences as Courbet, and also to the landscapists of the Barbizon school. The fourth includes followers of the impressionists, the *pointillistes*, the symbolists, the post-impressionists, and other recent movements in French painting. Nevertheless, with some exceptions, the Belgian painters have a decided national character of their own.

The first period unites to the romanticism of 1830 something of the technique and the large manner of Rubens; but it is impossible to-day to be enthusiastic over many of its examples. The ambitious painter who inaugurated it, Wappers, was a lover of large designs; and the rest of his school—artists such as De Keyzer, Gallait, and Slingeneyer—vied with one another in the size of their compositions. Their vast canvases, crowded with life-size figures, have a physical prominence in the Brussels gallery of modern painting which can easily give the casual

H

visitor a false impression of Belgian art as a whole. Yet by making the great epochs of Flemish, Brabant, and Burgundian history live again before the eyes of the emancipated people, these men of the 'thirties and 'forties played their part in the national revival. Contemporary with them, and sharing their apprenticeship to Rubens as well as their exaggerated cult of size, was Antoine Wiertz, whose work is preserved at Brussels in a separate collection. Wiertz had in him so much of the charlatan, and his appeal to the popular sight-seer has so largely been made on that side, that it is easy to overlook the quality of his more serious efforts and of his technique at its best.

The one great creative genius of this period was Henri Leys, who among the historical painters not only of Belgium, but of Europe, holds quite a unique place. Leys also learned his methods in his own country; though he went for them to the painters of the fifteenth and sixteenth centuries, particularly those of the Brabant school, from Roger Van der Weyden down to B. Van Orley and the elder Breughel. But the style which he developed was his own; and his subjects, mostly chosen from the period of the Reformation, are all transfused by his individual temperament, with its brooding vision, its deep sense of tragedy, and a sort of aristocratic reserve. Leys was a wealthy nobleman; he painted to please nobody but himself; and he transmitted to none of his imitators the secret of his originality.

In the succeeding period, of genre painting, the typical figures are Alfred Stevens and Henri de Braeckeleer. Stevens' development was purely Parisian. He learned his art in the school of the Second Empire, and carried sheer virtuosity in the use of the brush to a point at which all Paris worshipped it. But his achievement had as little to do with the Art of his native country—past, present, or future—as the Parisian ladies and Montmartre studios, which were the subjects of its cleverness, had to do with the scenes and people of Brabant or Flanders. The genius of De Braeckeleer, on the other hand, was essentially Belgian. His spiritual ancestor is David Teniers; but he was a man of his own time. His sunny Flemish interiors, the bright faces of his old people, and the happy romping of his children, are both original and national. They are something which he has seen, and could only have seen, just as they are, in his own country. He stands out over his period, as Leys does over his, each representing the point at which their respective schools touched immortality.

Contemporary with Stevens and De Braeckeleer was a remarkable artist, whom it is hard to place, Charles de Groux. He has been called a kind of Millet of the poor of great towns; and he depicted with much power and gloom the bareness, the hunger, the poignancy, and the tragedy of life under slum conditions. There is no exaggeration in De Groux; he was not a propagandist or a social reformer; but he felt with a simple directness the intense suffering of others, and rendered his feeling on canvas not less directly. His technique was extremely good, and some of its features, such as the black emphasis of outlines, have been commoner since than before; indeed, not the least remarkable feature of his painting is its date. Spiritually he is the forerunner of some of the best work done within the last generation.

The third period really opens with the advent about 1870 of the Naturalist School of the " Art Libre." The first leaders of this were the Walloons, Rops and Artan, and the Flemings, Eugène Smits and Verwée. Rops showed his forceful and somewhat acrid talent as an etcher. Artan stands out as the first of the Belgian sea-painters. Smits, with a Keatsian sense of what is authentic and permanent in Paganism, excelled in painting the figure. Verwée, who found his landscapes and cows in the pastoral portions of the great Belgian plain, was the most Flemish and the most naturalistic of the group. What distinguishes them all is their predilection for the open air; their striving to get clear, not only from the traditions of the studio, but even from its physical presence; their search for beauty in the world of natural objects, in the sea and the meadows and the rivers, the eternal youth of the forests and the illimitable horizons of the great plain. Perhaps Verwée, with his unique rendering of the spaces of Flanders, should be ranked as the most permanently successful.

The " Art Libre " unlocked floodgates of varied talent; and since then Belgian art has never run in a well-defined channel. The paintings of Constantin Meunier belong to this period; but though full of individuality they lack that mastery of the medium, which he afterwards attained as a sculptor. The initiator of the fourth period which we have described—and still in some ways its greatest figure—was Émile Claus. It is easy, and possibly true, to say that Claus would never have found his method if Claude Monet had not painted before him; nevertheless it is an individual method, and has brought something new into the world. No one before had shown with such immediacy the brilliant

colours of natural objects in sunlight—not
the sunlight of the Mediterranean coasts,
which quenches colours in its white glare,
but the clear temperate sunlight of Flanders,
which gives them their fullest possible value.
There is very little in M. Claus's landscapes
which is obtrusively local; yet when one
knows he is a native of Ghent, that region of
horticulture and flower-growing set in the
coloured and chequered Flemish plain, one
has an important key to his work. It has
had many imitators, but no rival.

The delicate study of light which forms the
basis of Claus's painting may be also seen in
the very different work of Verstraeten, in
whose landscapes there is a grave and melancholy note, echoing the more stoical emotions
of the race. Among many imitators of the
French *pointillistes*, one might mention Van
Rysselberghe as perhaps the most interesting.
Few Belgian painters show any trace of
English influence; but an exception might be
made of F. Knopff, a very clever eclectic who
owes a little to the Pre-Raphaelites. In a
category by itself comes the work of Jean
Delville, whose classic forms and imaginative
idealism have had some vogue outside Belgium.
But the most considerable Belgian painter
since Émile Claus is Léon Frédéric, a Walloon,
who depicts the bald cultivated landscapes

that lie between the towns of the South, and the hard patient life of their toilers. He has worked out a technique of his own, peculiarly adapted to his subjects; and there is a depth of perception in his treatment of labour which brings his painting at times into the region of Meunier's sculpture. But whereas in Meunier the tragedy of the worker is always accompanied by a sense of exultation in his strength, in Frédéric the impression is of pity and hardship only.

In this brief sketch of Belgian painting we have mentioned but few names, and omitted many which have deservedly a high national reputation; nor has anything been said of the very latest aspirants to public notice, whose claims are still being canvassed and disputed. It is difficult in short compass to give an adequate idea of the fertility of Belgian painting. Of course, neither Antwerp, Brussels, nor Ghent, can compare, as an international Art centre, with Paris or Rome; but the Belgian nation is, in proportion to its size, producing far more painting—and more good painting—than the French, or indeed any contemporary nation. Cosmopolitanism and the influence of Paris, which is geographically so near, are a certain danger for it, as they are for Belgian literature. The Royal Academy of Fine Arts at Antwerp has rendered valuable service in preserving a national tradition; but the real basis of this tradition must be sought in the multitude of masterpieces, which are scattered everywhere through the towns, in churches, public galleries, and private collections.

In sculpture, unlike painting, the country has nothing great to show before the nineteenth century; but since 1830 it has come gradually to take an important place. The sculptors of the first two generations were mediocre and conscientious artists, who owed whatever merit they possessed to Paris. But about the time when the " Art Libre " flooded Belgian painting, a new life came into sculpture also. In the work of Paul de Vigne grace and beauty are expressed with a certain real distinction; and the same qualities, with an added power and originality, characterise the remarkable sculptor, C. Vanderstappen. The vigorous and racy groups of Jef Lambeaux come later; and on the threshold of the twentieth century special mention is due to the genius of Julien Dillens, prematurely cut off, whose figures for tombs and cemeteries attain a rare and pure pathos by very simple and solely sculptural means. But by far the greatest artist in Belgian sculpture stands outside this succession. Constantin Meunier, to whom we briefly alluded above, began life as a painter; and it was not till he was past middle age that he turned seriously to the sister art. He then struck out an entirely original vein : and studying the living forms of the workers, whom he saw round him in the Walloon district—coal-heavers, iron-puddlers, glass-blowers, stone-cutters, and the like—he made himself the sculptor of modern labour. The power and spontaneity of his conceptions is matched by a masterly execution; and the body of work which he left at his death was such as no nineteenth-century sculptor, excepting M. Rodin, has equalled. This work is still quite insufficiently known in England and America; where indeed there has been scarcely any opportunity of seeing it. But it may be safely asserted that the better it is known, the more highly it will rank; among competent critics it has never encountered a dissentient voice. Modern Belgian art has scarcely produced anything greater; but it stands quite by itself, apart from almost the whole artistic tradition of the nation. This may be because the tradition is essentially Flemish, and Meunier is essentially Walloon. Throughout Flemish painting—and the same is true of Flemish architecture, with the single exception of the Cloth Hall at Ypres—there is a marked lack of that clear, logical unity of conception and structure, which one admires, for instance, in the greatest buildings of the French Gothic. Meunier has this quality, so peculiarly necessary for the highest sculpture; so that if you were to knock a head or an arm off one of his figures, it would, like a Greek statue, remain living and eloquent.

Meunier has left behind him at least one able disciple, Victor Rousseau. He has done some remarkable work; but he lacks the originating genius of his master.

If we turn now to Belgian literature, we find it bisected by the barrier of languages. There is a French literature, and a Flemish literature. There is even a third, a Walloon literature; but regarding the last it may be sufficient to remark that though a good deal has been printed in this curious speech, it scarcely seems to have produced a Mistral or a Burns with claims on the wider European public. French was declared the official language by the Constitution of 1830; and it was then, as it is now, spoken by the upper classes throughout Belgium. It had been spoken in Flanders since the Middle Ages; and the old aristocracy were quite content. The workers had less reason to be. It was not till 1873, that a Flemish prisoner charged with crime could be tried in any but the French language, however ignorant of it he might personally be. The law redressing this hardship was followed in 1878 by one which directed all official announcements in the Flemish-speaking provinces to be issued in Flemish, or in the two languages. Flemish has now long enjoyed equality in the elementary schools; and one of the aims of *flamingantisme* is to secure a similar equality in higher and even university education. But to this ambition it must be confessed that the practical objections from the standpoint of commerce and science seem to be considerable.

Between 1830 and 1870 there was much book-making in French, but little literature. Men wrote industriously about Belgian politics, Belgian antiquities, the forgotten glories of Belgian history, and so forth. Their work covered, with less distinction, the ground of the historical painters. It was not till 1857 that the first book of genius appeared. Charles de Coster (1827–79) was a civil servant, the son of a Liége man. He immersed himself in the Flemish lore of the fifteenth and sixteenth centuries and was also a keen student of Rabelais and Montaigne. He held that the spirit of old Flanders could not be expressed in modern French, and wrote the best of his works in the French of their period. These were *Légendes flamandes* (1857), and the *Légende de Thyl Uylenspiegel et de Lamme Goedzak*

(1867). The latter is really a national prose epic. Its full recognition was deferred for many years, till it was translated into modern French and Flemish; but there can be no doubt now that it is a very important work, entirely native in its inspiration. Thyl is an incarnation of the soul of the Flemish people; and the story of his resurrection was taken as a parable of its destiny. But De Coster died in poverty and discouragement; most of his glory has been posthumous. The only writer of genius among his Belgian contemporaries was Octave Pirmez; the author of tales and reflections more French in their affinities, with an air of proud melancholy and autumnal passion recalling Vigny or Chateaubriand.

So far as regards writings in the French language, the main movement in Belgian literature did not get under weigh till a decade after the rejuvenation of painting by the " Art Libre." Its pioneers were Camille Lemonnier, Edmond Picard, and Victor Arnould. In 1882 Picard founded the review *L'Art Moderne ;* and about the same time there appeared a number of similar periodicals, *La Jeune Belgique, La Wallonie,* and *La Société Nouvelle,* which combined with it to create a new literary impulse. Lemonnier, a Fleming, born in 1844, had published his first book, *Nos Flamands*, in 1869; but *Un Mâle* (1881) and *Le Mort* (1882) are probably his masterpieces. His long and fecund literary life extended into the twentieth century; and his late novels, *Adam et Ève* (1899) and *Au Cœur Frais de la Forêt* (1901), preaching a return to nature, are not the least striking of his books. In his different novels he studied types of all classes and regions in Belgium; he was a realist, a naturalist, a romanticist, and a symbolist by turns; and his essays in literary and artistic criticism, as well as those descriptive of Belgian localities, had an awakening influence on his countrymen. His prose style is somewhat extravagant, but embodies the national qualities of colour and force. Picard was a different, but admirable type. A leader of the Belgian Bar, the main author of the most learned of Belgian law-books, an active politician and later a representative of the Socialist party in the Senate, he was far too busy to become a very great writer; though some of his short novels, *La Forge Roussel* or *L'Amiral*, are still worth reading as the expression of a deep and powerful mind. But as a literary critic he had a rare gift for discerning the talents of others and stimulating their best use. No one did more than he to assert Belgian national independence in the field of literature. Arnould, an able reviewer, seconded his work.

The new school has produced both prose-writers and poets. Of the former the most noticeable, beside those already mentioned, are Eekhoud and G. Rodenbach. Eekhoud, born in 1854 in the Campine near Antwerp, is the most Flemish of the group. The heroes of his novels (the best known perhaps are *Kees Doorik* and *Les Kermesses*) are usually vagabonds, outlaws, ne'er-do-wells, the failures of life; the atmosphere is one of penetrating and somewhat benumbing tragedy. Georges Rodenbach (1855–98) was less autochthonous. He went early to Paris, and sat at the feet of Edmond de Goncourt. He wrote poetry, which shows the influence of Coppee and Sully-Prudhomme. It was only towards the end of his life that his mind reverted to his native Flanders. But the prose which he then produced, especially *Bruges la Morte* (1892), is a peculiarly delicate evocation of the spirit of the dead Flemish cities, the more delicate because not written in their presence, but distilled through the processes of memory. A more cheerful art steeped in romance and folklore, not dwelling on the death of these cities but re-animating their ancient life, is that of Eugène Demolder.

With two exceptions, the numerous poets

of the movement have produced little that lives. Giraud, Iwan Gilkin, Valère Gille, disciples of the French Parnassians and Baudelaire, Fernand Séverin, follower of Racine—they are interesting but minor bards. Among the very latest writers one or two have risen who may do more permanent work. But the figures which at present stand out still unrivalled are those of Émile Verhaeren and Maurice Maeterlinck. Verhaeren, born near Antwerp in 1855, and a school friend of Rodenbach at Ghent, was an active protagonist of the movement in the reviews of the 'eighties. The first stage of his poetry, typified by *Les Flamandes* (1883) and *Les Moines* (1886), is characterised by robust impressionism running to violence, the verse still remaining within regular French metres. With *Les Soirs* (1887) and other volumes, we pass to psychological studies; and in the next decade with *Campagnes hallucinées* (1893) and *Les Villes Tentaculaires* (1895), the poet attains his full strength. Technically he has liberated himself from most of the conventions of the French lyric, and developed an organ-music of his own; keeping closer to the sentence-accent of the spoken word, and piling up massive effects by means of assonances and rhymes within the lines. At the same time the personalities of his verse cease to be individuals; they become, first towns, villages, fields, and then those tendencies and processes of society, in whose tentacles the individual is held. The drained countryside, the vampire cities, the energy and ugliness of industrialism, the speeding-up of humanity's pace, all the ferment and baffled idealism of our time, sound in this poetry. There is yet a further stage, typified by *Les forces tumultueuses* (1901), of revolutionary vehemence and semi-prophetic declamation. Verhaeren has also written plays; but his genius is essentially lyrical and rhetorical. He remains a Fleming through his French medium; he has the instinct of his race for mysticism and symbolism, as well as for sensuous colour and riotous force. His verse is like a rich shell, through which winds blow; but they are not the usual poetic winds breathing from the spice-laden islands of the past, but the surging blinding tempests of the present and the future. No poet of our age has kept closer together the spheres of actuality and vision.

Verhaeren's work is untranslatable; and while it has been much appreciated in France, and still more perhaps in Germany, the English-speaking public, very few of whom can understand poetry in the French language, have left him practically unread. Very

different is the case of Maeterlinck, whose
prose, whether in his plays or his essays,
is singularly easy both to read and to trans-
late. Though he is an heir of the Flemish
mystics and his work is heavily charged
with symbols, the peculiarity of his method
is to express these not by strange words or
phrases, but by strange successions of the
simplest phrases. His first volume, *Serres
Chaudes* (1889), which Tolstoy's *What is
Art?* assailed as the last word in decadence,
shows the influence of Verlaine (himself of
Belgian descent); but the series of symbolistic
plays, culminating in *Pelléas et Mélisande*
(1892) and *Aglavaine et Sélysette* (1896),
developed an entirely original method. Since
then Maeterlinck's genius has evolved along
two main paths; one, that of a broader
and less shadow-haunted drama (*Monna
Vanna, Joyzelle,* and *The Blue Bird*), the
other, that of the semi-philosophical prose-
essays, of which *Le Trésor des Humbles*
(1896) was the first. His work is so well
known both in England and in America
that we need not here describe it more fully :
but it is worth pointing out its complete independence of French traditions. He derives
something from the Greeks; much from
the Flemish mystic, Ruysbroeck; something
from the Elizabethan dramatists; some-

thing from Novalis; but nothing whatever from Corneille or Racine, nor yet from Victor Hugo or the Parnassians. Working in the French language, he has wrought out something entirely un-French, which could only have been produced by a Belgian.

This last formula is necessarily that of the whole school. The Belgian nation is a different one, in some ways very different, from the French. If it uses the same language—and there are some obvious advantages in doing so—it must use it differently. The genius of France, as shown in her literature ever since Louis XIV, is distinguished ¦above all by its lucidity, elegance, lightness, precision, and wit. The Flemish genius, as it showed itself to the world in the Primitive painters, and later in the age of Rubens, is heavier and coarser, but in some ways richer, more powerful, more coloured. By a strange paradox it has always combined a strong animalism with a mystic spirituality. An author in modern Belgium is indeed in something of a dilemma. If he writes in French, he uses an instrument which was fashioned for other purposes than his, and cannot be made to do his work (if at all) without a certain violence. On the other hand if he writes in Flemish, which takes more naturally the colour of his temperament, he can only be understood by a small circle of readers; and for such purposes as science or philosophy he would have either to borrow Dutch or largely to create his language as he went along. At present, to write an original treatise on political economy or electricity in Flemish would be almost like writing one in the Dorset dialect. The French-speaking Belgians, with their distinguished publicists— Émile de Laveleye, Ernest Nys, and the rest—and their virtual monopoly of serious political oratory in the Chamber and the Senate, have here a great advantage over their Flemish-speaking fellow-countrymen. Yet in the realm of pure literature it is possible that the latter, though their fit audience be indeed few, have in some instances gone higher.

Flanders after 1830 underwent for many years an economic depression, due first to the closing of the Schelde and then to the potato disease. But in this period it produced two writers such as it had not known for centuries. Hendrik Conscience, of Ghent, published his first great novel *In't Wonderjaar 1566* in 1837, and *The Lion of Flanders* (describing the battle of the Golden Spurs) soon afterwards. These historical romances, based in form on Sir Walter Scott,

are works of undeniable power and passion :
and from them dates the Flemish awakening.
Their effect was continued and heightened
by the publication in 1843 of *Die Drie Zuster-
steden*, by Ledeganck, also of Ghent. His
poems on the " three sister towns " of Ghent,
Bruges and Antwerp, had not only very
great poetical merit, but they made a powerful appeal to Flemish patriotism, and against
the adoption of French ideas, manners, and
language. Ledeganck died in 1846; but
Conscience went on writing, and produced
novels of contemporary Flemish life (the
best, *The Conscript*, dates from 1850) scarcely
inferior to his historical romances. The
sudden appearance of a great prose-writer
and a great poet side by side in a small
and backward country, as Flanders then
was, is a phenomenon not easy to explain.
There was nothing like it at the time in the
literature of Holland, still less in the French
literature of Belgium. Neither Conscience
nor Ledeganck had the delicacy of style
achieved by some of their successors; but
the breadth and strength of their writing
would have won a European reputation,
could Europe have read it.

A considerable school arose with and
after them—J. T. Van Ryswyck, a writer
of political and satirical songs; Van Duyse,

copious author of odes, plays and books, who occasionally reached high quality; Damien Sleeckx (1818–1901) of Antwerp, realistic novelist. But the greatest of all Flemish poets—possibly, though no foreigner can make a comparison with confidence, of all Belgian writers—appeared rather later, in West Flanders. Guido Gezelle was a priest and teacher at a Church secondary school in the out-of-the-way town of Roulers. He took the picturesque and virginal West-Flemish speech, which he spoke and heard, and made of it a new poetic style, perfect in its blend of spontaneity and art. He was a poet of the inner life, immortalising little things and casting round daily incidents an atmosphere of emotion and beauty. Some of his lyrics have been compared to Verlaine; but he has not Verlaine's diseased nerves; he is more wholesome and more human. In 1860, after his first poems were published, but before they were widely known, he fell into ecclesiastical disgrace, and was dismissed from his post at Roulers. The facts are obscure, but his spirit was so deeply stricken and humiliated that for thirty years he practically wrote nothing. Meanwhile, towards the 'eighties, his poetry found disciples, the ablest of whom was Albrecht Rodenbach (1857–81), tragically cut off by consumption from a career of great promise. After the earlier 'eighties the leader of the Flemish literary movement was a third eminent poet, Pol de Mont, of Antwerp. Utilising the technique of his predecessors, he brought in from foreign, chiefly French, sources quite a new current of modernity, " art for Art's sake," and sensuous beauty. But in the middle of Pol de Mont's reign the aged Gezelle issued from his long silence; and in 1892 and 1895 published a series of poems of old age, of an almost rarer beauty than those by which he had hitherto been known. At the same time his nephew, Styn Streuvels, a humble baker of Avelghem, suddenly appeared as a novelist, with a prose style only less of a revelation than his uncle's poetry. Streuvel's books have a simple realism, recalling the technique of the Russian novel; but with no Russian subtlety of analysis. Their great merit is their style; and like Gezelle's poetry they are untranslatable.

This brief sketch of a little-known movement may serve to explain some of the spiritual force which there is behind *flamingantisme*. The Flemish authors are much read and admired in Holland; but the Dutch and the Flemish, as we have repeatedly observed, are by no means one nation. The idiosyncrasy of Gezelle and Streuvels is no more that of Amsterdam than their idiom is;

they can appreciate each other as foreigners
only.   Hence the desire of Catholic Flanders,
that its language should not remain trampled
underfoot as a mere *patois ;* a laudable
desire, and yet one to which natural, not legal,
inequalities present to-day the chief obstacle.

Besides painting, sculpture, and imaginative literature, there is much attention
given in modern Belgium to the arts of music
and architecture. It is sometimes said that
music is the special art of the Walloons, as
painting is of the Flemings. Certainly in the
Walloon country, as in Wales, there is a great
amount of popular music—choral societies,
orchestral societies, etc.—among the workmen.
The great composers, like César Franck, and
the great executants, like M. Ysaÿe, are usually
Walloons by extraction. But the love of music
extends all over the country.   One of the first
things to which local politicians attend,
whether Catholic, Liberal, or Socialist, is the
organisation of a band.   Musical education is
well provided for. The State keeps up four
Royal Conservatoires of music—at Brussels,
Antwerp, Liége, and Ghent—at which the
highest grades of teaching are made available for over 5000 pupils.   It also supports
a number of schools of music in all the
provinces, with pupils numbering another
15,000. It subsidises opera both in Brussels

and Antwerp; and the large opera-house in the capital, with its excellent and cheap performances of the best works (which with rare exceptions are always given in French, the language of the city), has made music-drama a popular art in Belgium, while in England and the United States it remains for the most part a fashionable exotic. Young composers are plentiful in Belgium; but since César Franck the country has thrown up no outstanding creative musical genius.

Architecture in Belgium shows through the centuries a certain continuity of aim. With only a few exceptions, the great mediæval buildings in its cities are relatively late; and though they are very beautiful, it is the beauty of florid ornament and architectural rhetoric rather than that of structural ideas. The builders of the last half-century, working mostly in Renaissance styles, fall still more easily into this habit. The exceptionally fine building-stones, which are quarried in the Namur province and elsewhere, lend themselves to the rhetoric of the orders. Among all the great public buildings in modern Belgium there is only one that reveals qualities much beyond these; and it is fortunate, that it happens to be the largest, the costliest, and the most conspicuous. This is the Palais de Justice at Brussels, designed by Poelaert and completed in 1883. It is placed on a magnificent site, of which its elevations are designed to take the greatest advantage; and anyone familiar with modern Brussels need only try to see it in his mind's eye with these elevations left out, in order to realise the effect which they have on the appearance of the whole city. But the Palace is praise-worthy not only for this and for Poelaert's impressive adaptation of Egyptian motives, but for a masterly plan and highly original solutions of the problem of internal lighting. With this exception, the modern public buildings of Belgium, though numerous and imposing, are somewhat lacking in originality. French, American, and latterly German ideas have been freely drawn upon, and the mixed Renaissance and steel-girder styles of the later nineteenth and the twentieth centuries are well represented. While the merit of this architecture is purely selective, it is nevertheless considerable. The fine modern parts of the Belgian cities are as fine as any in Europe; and it is impossible not to admire the vigour with which their authorities have cleared congested sites and created thoroughfares and boulevards. There has been no meticulous town-planning to compare with that in Germany; but the Burgo-masters possess, *ex-officio*, great powers over

structures; and the outward development
of the larger cities has been better controlled
and designed than in England or France. The
people have something like a national gift for
laying out ground and buildings effectively;
and their passion for handsome edifices has in
the last forty years become almost unbridled.
There have been two special incentives to it.
One is the low cost of building in Belgium,
which is little more than half that in Britain.
The other was the personal influence of Leopold
II, who had a taste for architecture and the
laying-out of ground, which he evinced for no
other art. Not only did he always encourage
public bodies in such enterprises, but towards
the end of his life he spent enormous sums
from his own Congo profits on carrying out
immense schemes of this kind at Brussels,
Tervueren, Ostend, and elsewhere.

How much will escape the devastation
of the European War, it is impossible to
the time of writing to prophesy. But in
any case the first sequel of peace in Belgium
must be rebuilding. It will be fortunate then,
that in consequence of the building fever of
recent years the country is equipped beyond
the ordinary needs of its size with architects,
builders, trained workmen, and experience,
which may enable its ruined towns to rise
purified and beautified from their ashes.

BIBLIOGRAPHY

I. In English

LAND AND LABOUR: LESSONS FROM BELGIUM. By
B. Seebohm Rowntree. London: 1910.

By far the best English book on Belgium. The author has
made an exhaustive study of many of the social problems of
modern Belgium; for which he not only consulted every
existing source of information, but conducted an original
investigation on a large scale and by the latest scientific
methods.

A HISTORY OF BELGIUM. By Demetrius C. Boulger.
London: Part I, 1902; Part II, 1909.

A useful account of Belgian history from Julius Cæsar to
the death of Leopold I. It seems to be based mainly on
M. Théodore Juste's work, for which see below.

BELGIUM OF THE BELGIANS. By Demetrius C. Boulger.
London: 1911.

A popular description of the country by the same author.

BELGIUM: HER KINGS, KINGDOM, AND PEOPLE. By
J. de C. MacDonnell. London: 1914.

Contains clever character-sketches of Leopold I, Leopold
II, and King Albert; with an account of Belgian politics
from the standpoint of the Catholic party.

BELGIUM THE LAND OF ART. By W. E. Griffis. New York:
1912.

A popular book for sight-seers; but gives some account of
the modern progress of the country.

CONSULAR REPORTS.

The Reports of the British Consul-General, Sir Cecil
Hertslet, are always exceedingly well done. The latest
Report on Belgium as a whole was published in 1913; the
latest on the Port of Antwerp in 1914.

REFERENCE BOOKS.

The *Statesman's Year Book* and *Bædeker's Guide to Belgium
and Holland* will give the English reader much statistical
and topographical information which he could not obtain
elsewhere.

II. In French

HISTOIRE DE BELGIQUE. By Prof. H. Pirenne (of Ghent
University). Brussels: Vol. I, 1900; Vol. II, 1903;
Vol. III, 1907; Vol. IV, 1911.

A work embodying the latest modern scholarship. The
last volume carries it down to the year 1648.

LES ANCIENNES DÉMOCRATIES DES PAYS-BAS. By the same author. Paris : 1910.

A brilliant sketch of the period of the communes.

HISTOIRE DE BELGIQUE. By Théodore Juste. Best edition, 3 vols. Brussels : 1895.

The best-known Belgian history of Belgium. M. Juste, a prolific writer, also published monographs on the leaders of the Revolution of 1830 which throw many sidelights on that event.

HISTOIRE DE FLANDRE. By Baron J. M. B. C. Kervyn de Lettenhove. Third edition, 4 vols. Brussels : 1874.

JACQUES D'ARTEVELDE. By the same. Second edition. Ghent : 1863.

Baron J. M. B. C. Kervyn de Lettenhove was the most brilliant Belgian historical writer during the nineteenth century. Besides embodying much research, his work has literary merit. It is sometimes over-coloured by Catholic sympathies.

LA BELGIQUE MODERNE. By H. Charriaut. Paris : 1910.

A French study of Belgian society and politics ; it covers readably a good deal of ground, but its judgments are superficial.

ÉCHOS DES LUTTES CONTEMPORAINES. By Charles Woeste. 2 vols. Brussels : 1906.

By the leader of uncompromising Conservatism in Belgium ; gives interesting presentment of the Conservative-Catholic position.

HISTOIRE DE LA DÉMOCRATIE ET DU SOCIALISME EN BELGIQUE. By Louis Bertrand. Brussels, 2 vols : 1906, 1907.

HISTOIRE DE LA COOPÉRATION EN BELGIQUE. By the same author. Brussels, 2 vols. : 1901, 1904.

Two books by one of the best-known Socialist leaders. The first is a history of Belgian Socialism ; the second, that of its Co-operative Stores.

L'EXODE RURAL ET LE RETOUR AUX CHAMPS. By Émile Vandervelde. Brussels : 1903.

A brilliant study, by the ablest of the Belgian Socialists, of the interactions between town and country in Belgium ; it examines particularly the social consequences of the system of cheap workmen's tickets.

La Belgique Ouvrière. By the same author. Paris: 1906.

A compact description of working-class Belgium, written for the French public.

Modernités. By Pol de Mont. Brussels: 1911.

An anthology of Belgian poetry written in the French language since 1880; compiled by the famous Flemish poet and art-critic.

Official Reports.

There is a Central Statistical Commission, which issues official statistics. Reports of departmental work are also published by the Departments of the Interior, Agriculture, Waters and Forests, Railways, Posts and Telegraphs, Instruction, Industry and Labour. The *Annuaire du Commerce et de l'Industrie de Belgique*, published annually by A. Mertens, Brussels, is quasi-official.

Periodicals.

Ably conducted reviews in Belgium tend to be of common occurrence, but short-lived. Some of the best intellectual work is to be found in back numbers of dead magazines. One might mention on the side of art and literature *L'Art Moderne* (1881–1887) and *La Jeune Belgique* (1881–1897); and on the side of sociology the *Annales de l'Institut des Sciences Sociales* (1894–1900).

INDEX

PRINTED IN GREAT BRITAIN BY RICHARD CLAY & SONS, LIMITED,
BRUNSWICK ST., STAMFORD ST., S.E., AND BUNGAY, SUFFOLK.

The
Home University
Library of Modern Knowledge

A Comprehensive Series of New and Specially Written Books

EDITORS :
PROF. GILBERT MURRAY, D.Litt., LL.D., F.B.A.
HERBERT FISHER, LL.D., F.B.A.
PROF. J. ARTHUR THOMSON, M.A., LL.D.
PROF. WILLIAM T. BREWSTER, M.A.

1/- net in cloth	256 Pages	2/6 net in leather

History and Geography

3. THE FRENCH REVOLUTION

By HILAIRE BELLOC, M.A. (With Maps.) "It is coloured with all the militancy of the author's temperament."—*Daily News*.

4. A SHORT HISTORY OF WAR AND PEACE

By G. H. PERRIS. The Rt. Hon. JAMES BRYCE writes : "I have read it with much interest and pleasure, admiring the skill with which you have managed to compress so many facts and views into so small a volume."

8. POLAR EXPLORATION

By Dr W. S. BRUCE, F.R.S.E., Leader of the "Scotia" Expedition. (With Maps.) "A very freshly written and interesting narrative."—*The Times*.

12. THE OPENING-UP OF AFRICA

By Sir H. H. JOHNSTON, G.C.M.G., F.Z.S. (With Maps.) "The Home University Library is much enriched by this excellent work."—*Daily Mail*.

13. MEDIÆVAL EUROPE

By H. W. C. DAVIS, M.A. (With Maps.) "One more illustration of the fact that it takes a complete master of the subject to write briefly upon it."—*Manchester Guardian*.

14. THE PAPACY & MODERN TIMES (1303-1870)

By WILLIAM BARRY, D.D. "Dr Barry has a wide range of knowledge and an artist's power of selection."—*Manchester Guardian*.

23. HISTORY OF OUR TIME (1885–1911)

By G. P. GOOCH, M.A. "Mr Gooch contrives to breathe vitality into his story, and to give us the flesh as well as the bones of recent happenings."—*Observer.*

25. THE CIVILISATION OF CHINA

By H. A. GILES, LL.D., Professor of Chinese at Cambridge. "In all the mass of facts, Professor Giles never becomes dull. He is always ready with a ghost story or a street adventure for the reader's recreation."—*Spectator.*

29. THE DAWN OF HISTORY

By J. L. MYRES, M.A., F.S.A., Wykeham Professor of Ancient History, Oxford. "There is not a page in it that is not suggestive."—*Manchester Guardian.*

33. THE HISTORY OF ENGLAND

A Study in Political Evolution
By Prof. A. F. POLLARD, M.A. With a Chronological Table. "It takes its place at once among the authoritative works on English history."—*Observer.*

34. CANADA

By A. G. BRADLEY. "The volume makes an immediate appeal to the man who wants to know something vivid and true about Canada."—*Canadian Gazette.*

37. PEOPLES & PROBLEMS OF INDIA

By Sir T. W. HOLDERNESS, K.C.S.I., Permanent Under-Secretary of State of the India Office. "Just the book which newspaper readers require to-day, and a marvel of comprehensiveness."—*Pall Mall Gazette.*

42. ROME

By W. WARDE FOWLER, M.A. "A masterly sketch of Roman character and of what it did for the world."—*The Spectator.*

48. THE AMERICAN CIVIL WAR

By F. L. PAXSON, Professor of American History, Wisconsin University. (With Maps.) "A stirring study."—*The Guardian.*

51. WARFARE IN BRITAIN

By HILAIRE BELLOC, M.A. "Rich in suggestion for the historical student."—*Edinburgh Evening News.*

55. MASTER MARINERS

By J. R. SPEARS. "A continuous story of shipping progress and adventure... It reads like a romance."—*Glasgow Herald.*

61. NAPOLEON

By HERBERT FISHER, LL.D., F.B.A., Vice-Chancellor of Sheffield University. (With Maps.) The story of the great Bonaparte's youth, his career, and his downfall, with some sayings of Napoleon, a genealogy, and a bibliography.

66. THE NAVY AND SEA POWER

By DAVID HANNAY. The author traces the growth of naval power from early times, and discusses its principles and effects upon the history of the Western world.

71. GERMANY OF TO-DAY

By CHARLES TOWER. "It would be difficult to name any better summary."—*Daily News.*

82. PREHISTORIC BRITAIN

By ROBERT MUNRO, M.A., M.D., LL.D., F.R.S.E. (Illustrated.)

91. THE ALPS

By ARNOLD LUNN, M.A. (Illustrated.)

92. CENTRAL & SOUTH AMERICA

By Professor W. R. SHEPHERD. (Maps.

97. *THE ANCIENT EAST*

By D. G. HOGARTH, M.A. (Maps.)

98. *THE WARS between ENGLAND and AMERICA*

By Prof. T. C. SMITH.

100. *HISTORY OF SCOTLAND*

By Prof. R. S. RAIT.

Literature and Art

2. *SHAKESPEARE*

By JOHN MASEFIELD. "We have had more learned books on Shakespeare in the last few years, but not one so wise."—*Manchester Guardian.*

27. *ENGLISH LITERATURE: MODERN*

By G. H. MAIR, M.A. "Altogether a fresh and individual book."—*Observer.*

35. *LANDMARKS IN FRENCH LITERATURE*

By G. L. STRACHEY. "It is difficult to imagine how a better account of French Literature could be given in 250 small pages."—*The Times.*

39. *ARCHITECTURE*

By Prof. W. R. LETHABY. (Over forty Illustrations.) "Delightfully bright reading."—*Christian World.*

43. *ENGLISH LITERATURE: MEDIÆVAL*

By Prof. W. P. KER, M.A. "Prof. Ker's knowledge and taste are unimpeachable, and his style is effective, simple, yet never dry."—*The Athenæum.*

45. *THE ENGLISH LANGUAGE*

By L. PEARSALL SMITH, M.A. "A wholly fascinating study of the different streams that make the great river of the English speech."—*Daily News.*

52. *GREAT WRITERS OF AMERICA*

By Prof. J. ERSKINE and Prof. W. P. TRENT. "An admirable summary, from Franklin to Mark Twain, enlivened by a dry humour."—*Athenæum.*

63. *PAINTERS AND PAINTING*

By Sir FREDERICK WEDMORE. (With 16 half-tone illustrations.) From the Primitives to the Impressionists.

64. *DR JOHNSON AND HIS CIRCLE*

By JOHN BAILEY, M.A. "A most delightful essay."—*Christian World.*

65. *THE LITERATURE OF GERMANY*

By Professor J. G. ROBERTSON, M.A., Ph.D. "Under the author's skilful treatment the subject shows life and continuity."—*Athenæum.*

70. *THE VICTORIAN AGE IN LITERATURE*

By G. K. CHESTERTON. "No one will put it down without a sense of having taken a tonic or received a series of electric shocks."—*The Times.*

73. *THE WRITING OF ENGLISH*

By W. T. BREWSTER, A.M., Professor of English in Columbia University. "Sensible, and not over-rigidly conventional."—*Manchester Guardian.*

75. *ANCIENT ART AND RITUAL.*

By JANE E. HARRISON, LL.D., D.Litt. "Charming in style and learned in manner."—*Daily News.*

76. EURIPIDES AND HIS AGE

By GILBERT MURRAY, D.Litt., LL.D., F.B.A., Regius Professor of Greek at Oxford. "A beautiful piece of work. . . . Just in the fulness of time, and exactly in the right place. . . . Euripides has come into his own."—*The Nation.*

87. CHAUCER AND HIS TIMES

By GRACE E. HADOW.

89. WILLIAM MORRIS: HIS WORK AND INFLUENCE

By A. CLUTTON BROCK.

93. THE RENAISSANCE

By EDITH SICHEL.

95. ELIZABETHAN LITERATURE

By J. M. ROBERTSON, M.P.

99. AN OUTLINE OF RUSSIAN LITERATURE

By Hon. MAURICE BARING.

Science

7. MODERN GEOGRAPHY

By DR MARION NEWBIGIN. (Illustrated.) "Geography, again : what a dull, tedious study that was wont to be ! . . . But Miss Marion Newbigin invests its dry bones with the flesh and blood of romantic interest."—*Daily Telegraph.*

9. THE EVOLUTION OF PLANTS

By Dr D. H. SCOTT, M.A., F.R.S., late Hon. Keeper of the Jodrell Laboratory, Kew. (Fully illustrated.) "Dr Scott's candid and familiar style makes the difficult subject both fascinating and easy."—*Gardeners' Chronicle.*

17. HEALTH AND DISEASE

By W. LESLIE MACKENZIE, M.D., Local Government Board, Edinburgh.

18. INTRODUCTION TO MATHEMATICS

By A. N. WHITEHEAD, Sc.D., F.R.S. (With Diagrams.) "Mr Whitehead has discharged with conspicuous success the task he is so exceptionally qualified to undertake. For he is one of our great authorities upon the foundations of the science."—*Westminster Gazette.*

19. THE ANIMAL WORLD

By Professor F. W. GAMBLE, F.R.S. With Introduction by Sir Oliver Lodge. (Many Illustrations.) "A fascinating and suggestive survey."—*Morning Post.*

20. EVOLUTION

By Professor J. ARTHUR THOMSON and Professor PATRICK GEDDES. "A many-coloured and romantic panorama, opening up, like no other book we know, a rational vision of world-development."—*Belfast News-Letter.*

22. CRIME AND INSANITY

By Dr C. A. MERCIER. "Furnishes much valuable information from one occupying the highest position among medico-legal psychologists."—*Asylum News.*

28. PSYCHICAL RESEARCH

By Sir W. F. BARRETT, F.R.S., Professor of Physics, Royal College of Science, Dublin, 1873-1910. "What he has to say on thought-reading, hypnotism, telepathy, crystal-vision, spiritualism, divinings, and so on, will be read with avidity."—*Dundee Courier.*

31. ASTRONOMY

By A. R. HINKS, M.A., Chief Assistant, Cambridge Observatory. "Original in thought, eclectic in substance, and critical in treatment. . . . No better little book is available."—*School World*.

32. INTRODUCTION TO SCIENCE

By J. ARTHUR THOMSON, M.A., Regius Professor of Natural History, Aberdeen University. "Professor Thomson's delightful literary style is well known; and here he discourses freshly and easily on the methods of science and its relations with philosophy, art, religion, and practical life."—*Aberdeen Journal*.

36. CLIMATE AND WEATHER

By Prof. H. N. DICKSON, D.Sc.Oxon., M.A., F.R.S.E., President of the Royal Meteorological Society. (With Diagrams.) "The author has succeeded in presenting in a very lucid and agreeable manner the causes of the movements of the atmosphere and of the more stable winds."—*Manchester Guardian*.

41. ANTHROPOLOGY

By R. R. MARETT, M.A., Reader in Social Anthropology in Oxford University. "An absolutely perfect handbook, so clear that a child could understand it, so fascinating and human that it beats fiction 'to a frazzle.'"—*Morning Leader*.

44. THE PRINCIPLES OF PHYSIOLOGY

By Prof. J. G. McKENDRICK, M.D. "Upon every page of it is stamped the impress of a creative imagination."—*Glasgow Herald*.

46. MATTER AND ENERGY

By F. SODDY, M.A., F.R.S. "Prof. Soddy has successfully accomplished the very difficult task of making physics of absorbing interest on popular lines."—*Nature*.

49. PSYCHOLOGY, THE STUDY OF BEHAVIOUR

By Prof. W. McDOUGALL, F.R.S., M.B. "A happy example of the non-technical handling of an unwieldy science, suggesting rather than dogmatising. It should whet appetites for deeper study."—*Christian World*.

53. THE MAKING OF THE EARTH

By Prof. J. W. GREGORY, F.R.S. (With 38 Maps and Figures.) "A fascinating little volume. . . . Among the many good things contained in the series this takes a high place."—*The Athenæum*.

57. THE HUMAN BODY

By A. KEITH, M.D., LL.D., Conservator of Museum and Hunterian Professor, Royal College of Surgeons. (Illustrated.) "It literally makes the 'dry bones' to live. It will certainly take a high place among the classics of popular science."—*Manchester Guardian*.

58. ELECTRICITY

By GISBERT KAPP, D.Eng., Professor of Electrical Engineering in the University of Birmingham. (Illustrated.) "It will be appreciated greatly by learners and by the great number of amateurs who are interested in what is one of the most fascinating of scientific studies."—*Glasgow Herald*.

62. THE ORIGIN AND NATURE OF LIFE

By Dr BENJAMIN MOORE, Professor of Bio-Chemistry, University College, Liverpool. "Stimulating, learned, lucid."—*Liverpool Courier*.

67. CHEMISTRY

By RAPHAEL MELDOLA, F.R.S., Professor of Chemistry in Finsbury Technical College, London. Presents clearly, without the detail demanded by the expert, the way in which chemical science has developed, and the stage it has reached.

72. PLANT LIFE

By Prof. J. B. FARMER, D.Sc., F.R.S. (Illustrated.) "Professor Farmer has contrived to convey all the most vital facts of plant physiology, and also to present a good many of the chief problems which confront investigators to-day in the realms of morphology and of heredity."—*Morning Post*.

78. THE OCEAN

A General Account of the Science of the Sea. By Sir JOHN MURRAY, K.C.B., F.R.S. (Colour plates and other illustrations.)

79. NERVES

By Prof. D. FRASER HARRIS, M.D., D.Sc. (Illustrated.) A description, in non-technical language, of the nervous system, its intricate mechanism and the strange phenomena of energy and fatigue, with some practical reflections.

86. SEX

By Prof. PATRICK GEDDES and Prof. J. ARTHUR THOMSON, LL.D. (Illus.)

88. THE GROWTH OF EUROPE

By Prof. GRENVILLE COLE. (Illus.)

Philosophy and Religion

---

15. MOHAMMEDANISM

By Prof. D. S. MARGOLIOUTH, M.A., D.Litt. "This generous shilling's worth of wisdom. . . . A delicate, humorous, and most responsible tractate by an illuminative professor."—*Daily Mail.*

40. THE PROBLEMS OF PHILOSOPHY

By the Hon. BERTRAND RUSSELL, F.R.S. "A book that the 'man in the street' will recognise at once to be a boon. . . . Consistently lucid and non-technical throughout."—*Christian World.*

47. BUDDHISM

By Mrs RHYS DAVIDS, M.A. "The author presents very attractively as well as very learnedly the philosophy of Buddhism."—*Daily News.*

50. NONCONFORMITY: Its ORIGIN and PROGRESS

By Principal W. B. SELBIE, M.A. "The historical part is brilliant in its insight, clarity, and proportion."—*Christian World.*

54. ETHICS

By G. E. MOORE, M.A., Lecturer in Moral Science in Cambridge University. "A very lucid though closely reasoned outline of the logic of good conduct." —*Christian World.*

56. THE MAKING OF THE NEW TESTAMENT

By Prof. B. W. BACON, LL.D., D.D. "Professor Bacon has boldly, and wisely, taken his own line, and has produced, as a result, an extraordinarily vivid, stimulating, and lucid book."—*Manchester Guardian.*

60. MISSIONS: THEIR RISE and DEVELOPMENT

By Mrs CREIGHTON. "Very interestingly done. . . . Its style is simple, direct, unhackneyed, and should find appreciation where a more fervently pious style of writing repels."—*Methodist Recorder.*

68. COMPARATIVE RELIGION

By Prof. J. ESTLIN CARPENTER, D.Litt., Principal of Manchester College, Oxford. "Puts into the reader's hand a wealth of learning and independent thought." —*Christian World.*

74. A HISTORY OF FREEDOM OF THOUGHT

By J. B. BURY, Litt.D., LL.D., Regius Professor of Modern History at Cambridge. "A little masterpiece, which every thinking man will enjoy." —*The Observer.*

84. LITERATURE OF THE OLD TESTAMENT

By Prof. GEORGE MOORE, D.D., LL.D., of Harvard. A detailed examination of the books of the Old Testament in the light of the most recent research.

90. THE CHURCH OF ENGLAND

By Canon E. W. WATSON, Regius Professor of Ecclesiastical History at Oxford.

94. RELIGIOUS DEVELOPMENT BETWEEN THE OLD AND NEW TESTAMENTS

By Canon R. H. CHARLES, D.D., D.Litt.

Social Science

1. PARLIAMENT

Its History, Constitution, and Practice. By Sir COURTENAY P. ILBERT, G.C.B., K.C.S.I., Clerk of the House of Commons. "The best book on the history and practice of the House of Commons since Bagehot's 'Constitution.'"—*Yorkshire Post.*

5. THE STOCK EXCHANGE

By F. W. HIRST, Editor of "The Economist." "To an unfinancial mind must be a revelation. . . . The book is as clear, vigorous, and sane as Bagehot's 'Lombard Street,' than which there is no higher compliment."—*Morning Leader.*

6. IRISH NATIONALITY

By Mrs J. R. GREEN. "As glowing as it is learned. No book could be more timely."—*Daily News.*

10. THE SOCIALIST MOVEMENT

By J. RAMSAY MACDONALD, M.P. "Admirably adapted for the purpose of exposition."—*The Times.*

11. CONSERVATISM

By LORD HUGH CECIL, M.A., M.P. "One of those great little books which seldom appear more than once in a generation."—*Morning Post.*

16. THE SCIENCE OF WEALTH

By J. A. HOBSON, M.A. "Mr J. A. Hobson holds an unique position among living economists. . . . Original, reasonable, and illuminating."—*The Nation.*

21. LIBERALISM

By L. T. HOBHOUSE, M.A., Professor of Sociology in the University of London. "A book of rare quality. . . . We have nothing but praise for the rapid and masterly summaries of the arguments from first principles which form a large part of this book."—*Westminster Gazette.*

24. THE EVOLUTION OF INDUSTRY

By D. H. MACGREGOR, M.A., Professor of Political Economy in the University of Leeds. "A volume so dispassionate in terms may be read with profit by all interested in the present state of unrest."—*Aberdeen Journal.*

26. AGRICULTURE

By Prof. W. SOMERVILLE, F.L.S. "It makes the results of laboratory work at the University accessible to the practical farmer."—*Athenæum.*

30. ELEMENTS OF ENGLISH LAW

By W. M. GELDART, M.A., B.C.L., Vinerian Professor of English Law at Oxford. "Contains a very clear account of the elementary principles underlying the rules of English Law."—*Scots Law Times.*

38. THE SCHOOL: An Introduction to the Study of Education.

By J. J. FINDLAY, M.A., Ph.D., Professor of Education in Manchester University. "An amazingly comprehensive volume. . . . It is a remarkable performance, distinguished in its crisp, striking phraseology as well as its inclusiveness of subject-matter."—*Morning Post.*

59. ELEMENTS OF POLITICAL ECONOMY

By S. J. CHAPMAN, M.A., Professor of Political Economy in Manchester University. "Its importance is not to be measured by its price. Probably the best recent critical exposition of the analytical method in economic science."—*Glasgow Herald.*

69. THE NEWSPAPER

By G. BINNEY DIBBLEE, M.A. (Illustrated.) The best account extant of the organisation of the newspaper press, at home and abroad.

77. SHELLEY, GODWIN, AND THEIR CIRCLE

By H. N. BRAILSFORD, M.A. "Mr Brailsford sketches vividly the influence of the French Revolution on Shelley's and Godwin's England; and the charm and strength of his style make his book an authentic contribution to literature."— *The Bookman.*

80. CO-PARTNERSHIP AND PROFIT-SHARING

By ANEURIN WILLIAMS, M.A. "A judicious but enthusiast history, with much interesting speculation on the future of Co-partnership."—*Christian World.*

81. PROBLEMS OF VILLAGE LIFE

By E. N. BENNETT, M.A. Discusses the leading aspects of the British land problem, including housing, small holdings, rural credit, and the minimum wage.

83. COMMON-SENSE IN LAW

By Prof. P. VINOGRADOFF, D.C.L.

85. UNEMPLOYMENT

By Prof. A. C. PIGOU, M.A.

96. POLITICAL THOUGHT IN ENGLAND: FROM BACON TO HALIFAX

By G. P. GOOCH, M.A.

IN PREPARATION

London : WILLIAMS AND NORGATE
And of all Bookshops and Bookstalls.